The

Wisdom *of* Proverbs, Job *and* Ecclesiastes

AN INTRODUCTION

TO WISDOM LITERATURE

Derek Kidner

IVP Academic

An imprint of InterVarsity Press
Downers Grove, Illinois

InterVarsity Press, USA
P.O. Box 1400, Downers Grove, IL 60515-1426, USA
World Wide Web: www.ivpress.com
Email: email@ivpress.com

Inter-Varsity Press, England
Norton Street, Nottingham NG7 3HR, England
Website: www.ivpbooks com
Email: ivp@ivpbooks.com

InterVarsity Press®, USA, is the book-publishing division of InterVarsity Christian Fellowship/USA®, a student movement active on campus at hundreds of universities, colleges and schools of nursing in the United States of America, and a member movement of the International Fellowship of Evangelical Students. For information about local and regional activities, write Public Relations Dept., InterVarsity Christian Fellowship/USA, 6400 Schroeder Rd., P.O. Box 7895, Madison, WI 53707-7895, or visit the IVCF website at <www.intervarsity.org>.

Inter-Varsity Press, England, is closely linked with the Universities and Colleges Christian Fellowship, a student movement connecting Christian Unions in universities and colleges throughout Great Britain, and a member movement of the International Fellowship of Evangelical Students. Website: www.uccf.org.uk.

Cover design: Cindy Kiple
Cover image. Mark Stay/ iStockphoto

Typeset in Century Schoolbook by Parker Typesetting Service, Leicester
Printed and bound in Great Britain by R. Clay (The Chaucer Press) Ltd., Bungay Suffolk

USA ISBN 978-0-87784-405-1

Printed in the United States of America ∞

Library of Congress Cataloging-in-Publication Data

Kidner, Derek.
   The wisdom of Proverbs, Job, and Ecclesiastes.

   Bibliography: p.
   Includes index.
   1. Bible. O.T. Proverbs—Criticism, interpretation, etc —History—20th century.
2. Bible. O.T Job—Criticism, interpretation, etc.—History—20th century. 3. Bible. O.T.
Ecclesiastes—Criticism, interpretation, etc.—History—20th century. 4. Wisdom
literature—Criticism, interpretation, etc.—History—20th century.
   I. Title.
BS1455.K53   1985   223'.06   85-11826

P   32   31   30   29   28   27   26   25
Y   21   20   19   18   17   16   15

Contents

Preface

For a lover of the Old Testament, few things could be more inviting than a call to explore and introduce its Wisdom books. So my first desire is to thank the Inter-Varsity Press for such a commission, as well as for their customary patience and care in getting the result into print.

To the reader I should explain that chapters 3, 5 and 7 are chiefly meant to give theological students a sample and assessment of the debate which has been sparked off by these books. The chapters can easily be skipped, and the threads be picked up in chapter 8: 'Voices in Counterpoint'.

My hope is that all this may whet the appetite for these scriptures themselves and for a thought-out godliness which has the steadiness of Proverbs, the resilience of Job and the sharp realism of Ecclesiastes. In a word, for wisdom not only to study but to live by.

DEREK KIDNER

Chief abbreviations

ANET   *Ancient Near Eastern Texts* edited by J. B. Prit-chard, ²1955, ³1969.

AV   Authorized Version (King James'), 1611.

BDB   *Hebrew-English Lexicon of the Old Testament* by F. Brown, S. R. Driver and C. A. Briggs, 1907.

BWANT   *Beiträge zur Wissenschaft vom alten (und neuen) Testament.*

BWL   *Babylonian Wisdom Literature* by W. G. Lambert (Oxford, 1960).

BZAW   *Beiheft zur Zeitschrift für die alttestamentliche Wissenschaft.*

CBQ   *Catholic Biblical Quarterly.*

DOTT   *Documents from Old Testament Times* edited by D. Winton Thomas, 1958.

EV   English versions.

GNB   Good News Bible (Today's English Version), 1976.

Heb.   Hebrew.

HUCA   *Hebrew Union College Annual.*

ICC   *International Critical Commentary.*

JB   Jerusalem Bible, 1966.

JBL   *Journal of Biblical Literature.*

LXX   The Septuagint (pre-Christian Greek Version of the Old Testament).

mg.   margin.

MT   Massoretic Text.

NEB   New English Bible, 1970.

NIV	New International Version, 1978.
RSV	Revised Standard Version, 1952.
RV	Revised Version, 1881.
SAIW	*Studies in Ancient Israelite Wisdom* edited by J. L. Crenshaw, 1976.
SJT	*Scottish Journal of Theology.*
Syr.	The Peshitta (Syriac Version of the Bible).
Tyn.B	*Tyndale Bulletin.*
VT	*Vetus Testamentum.*
VTS	*Supplements to Vetus Testamentum.*

1

A meeting of minds

A distinctive voice

There comes a point in the Old Testament when the pilgrim is free to stop and take a long look round. He has had a well-marked path to follow, and still it stretches on ahead. But now he must relate it to the world at large, to the scene spread out on every side: from what lies right at his feet (shrewdly pointed out in Proverbs) to what is barely visible at the horizon – the dark riddle of how the world is governed (the book of Job) and how it should be valued (Ecclesiastes).

'Now', says his guide, 'you see what sense it made to come the way we did – what false trails we avoided, what death-traps!'

'All the same', replies the pilgrim, 'there is plenty that I don't see; a lot that seems even wrong and pointless. Look at this, for instance, . . . and this . . . .'

In other words, in the Wisdom books the tone of voice and even the speakers have changed. The blunt 'Thou shalt' or 'shalt not' of the Law, and the urgent 'Thus saith the LORD' of the Prophets, are joined now by the cooler comments of the teacher and the often anguished questions of the learner. Where the bulk of the Old Testament calls us simply to obey and to believe, this part of it (chiefly the books we have mentioned, although wisdom is a thread that runs through every part) summons us to think hard as well as humbly; to keep our eyes open, to use our conscience and our common sense, and not to shirk the most disturbing questions.

The value of this approach

Simply as a form of teaching, this has something special for us. The lecture or the sermon, with its one-way flow, can make its points tidily and at leisure; but a lesson that draws the hearers into answering and asking, into working things out painfully, may well get further into the mind than any discourse, even if at times it deliberately leaves many questions unresolved.

Still more importantly, this demand for thought presupposes a world that answers to thought. Not, to be sure, one which we can hope to master with our finite minds; but that is our limitation, not the world's; for if it is a creation, and the product of perfect wisdom, it will be in principle intelligible. So even when the arrogance of human thought has to be rebuked (as we shall see), the Old Testament makes no retreat into notions of divine caprice; still less, of 'a tale told by an idiot' or by nobody at all. Instead, it sees God's wisdom expressed and echoed everywhere – except where man, the rebel, has presumed to disagree and to disrupt the pattern. This stamp of reason upon all God's works is something that the poets sing about with eloquence:

> Do you know the ordinances of the heavens? . . .
> Who has put wisdom in the clouds,
>   or given understanding to the mists?
>
> Jb. 38:33,36.

> Even the stork in the heavens
>   knows her times;
> and the turtledove, swallow, and crane
>   keep the time of their coming;
> but my people know not
>   the ordinance of the LORD. . . .
> Lo, they have rejected the word of the LORD,
>   and what wisdom is in them?
>
> Je. 8:7,9.

> The LORD by wisdom founded the earth;
>   by understanding he established the heavens . . .
>
> Pr. 3:19.

To put this in more prosaic terms, what is implied here is a single system, a universe; and what is invited is the study of it in a spirit of humility, so that we may take our due place within it willingly and intelligently. Certainly one way of exalting the Creator's glory is to dwell on his untrammelled choice of action, which makes all our calculations provisional:

> Our God is in the heavens;
> he does whatever he pleases
>
> Ps. 115:3.

And this, as Y. Kaufmann has reminded us, is no truism: it stands in utter contrast to the pagan view of deities who are limited by a pre-existent world-stuff or set of primeval powers, which are 'as independent and primary as the gods themselves', or are even the very source of their existence. 'To be sure,' adds Kaufmann, 'paganism has personal gods who create and govern the world of men. But a divine will, sovereign and absolute, which governs all and is the cause of all being – such a conception is unknown.'[1]

Yet the Old Testament ascribes to the sovereign LORD more than freedom. His creation *coheres*. Instead of a world order which is the unstable product of rival wills, as the mythologies suggest, and is therefore subject to the arbitrary pressures of magico-religious manipulation, the Old Testament sets the world before us as the harmonious composition of a single mind:

> O LORD, how manifold are thy works!
> In wisdom hast thou made them all.
>
> Ps. 104:24.

This is the faith in which the natural world can be confidently studied, whether by a simple observation of its patterns and its everyday sequences, such as are noted in Proverbs, or by the more rigorous techniques of modern science, both of which assume that reason can be fruitfully applied to the phenomena before us. It was no misuse of Scripture to inscribe over the entrance of not only the old Cavendish Laboratory in Cambridge but, in the 1970s, of the New Cavendish as well (this time in English, not Latin!), the words of Psalm 111:2 (AV),

> The works of the LORD are great,
> sought out of all them that have pleasure therein.

In this spirit Solomon, who had prayed for wisdom for the task of government and for discernment 'between good and evil' (1 Ki. 3:9), did not confine his thinking to these profes-

---

[1] Yehezkel Kaufmann, *The Religion of Israel* (translated and abridged by M. Greenberg; Allen & Unwin, 1961), pp.21f.

sionally useful realms, but 'spoke of trees . . . also of beasts, and of birds, and of reptiles, and of fish' (1 Ki. 4:33 [5:13, Heb.]). This makes common ground with the interests of all men. The presence of this kind of material in Scripture invites the man of God to study his whole environment, not simply that part of it which bears directly on the covenant or on morality. In these books he is aware of his fellow men as human beings rather than as Israelites or Gentiles; and when he turns to other creatures he can enjoy them with an artist's eye, noting for example their grace of movement or their skill in using their native elements. So he is taking God's creatorship as seriously as his redemption, and is giving due weight to the solidarity between 'all parts of his dominion', material and immaterial, measuring all alike by the single concept of wisdom – from the universe itself down to the behaviour of a colony of ants, or of a child or a courting couple, or of a buyer and seller doing business.

This has an immediate bearing on – at one extreme – the exclusive pietism which is a recurrent tendency within Christianity; and at another extreme, on the absolute autonomy which secularists claim for human culture – two opposite reactions against the crown rights of Deity, yet not dissimilar in their effects. The former would shut God *in* to the narrow circle of worship, ethics, evangelism and eschatology; the latter would shut God *out* of nine-tenths of the human scene, allowing him no voice in sociology, education, art or science, and allowing these realms no benefit of the Creator's mind and judgment.

The stimulus of Solomon

The opening of windows and doors towards the world at large, which Solomon's approach implies, did actually take place quite noticeably in his reign, which seems to have had something of the novelty and excitement that we associate with the Renaissance.[1] Israel's mental horizons, and in a sense her physical ones as well, were expanding. The king's ships, off and away into the Indian Ocean for three years at a time (1 Ki. 10:22), were trading, it seems, down the coast of Africa and across to India, returning with exotic cargoes of 'gold, silver, ivory, apes, and peacocks' (or baboons?); while overland the flow of goods was equally impressive and

---

[1]Some scholars reject this. Their objections are discussed in ch.3, below, pp.50ff.

very lucrative to a kingdom that sat astride the trade routes (see, *e.g.*, 1 Ki. 10:14–15, 29). With prosperity came the leisure and the fine materials to enrich the arts, and Solomon was quick to enlist the skills of foreigners wherever Israelite abilities fell short, whether in forestry or in the decorative arts or in seamanship (1 Ki. 5:6; 7:13–45; 9:27). In administration, too, there is some reason to think that Egyptian experience was drawn on for the task of running the greatly expanded kingdom that Solomon inherited from his father.[1] Everywhere there was a whirl of new activity.

Most significant of all, for our theme, was the spread of Solomon's intellectual fame, which drew the world to his door. The Queen of Sheba was but one of this stream of learned visitors, intent on trying out his erudition and wit. The queen's 'hard questions' were probably riddles in both senses of the word (Heb. *ḥîḏâ*) – at one level the kind of puzzle which Samson set his wedding guests in Judges 14:12ff., not unlike the teasing clues of a modern crossword; and at another level the dark enigmas of life, such as the riddle of unpunished evil which Psalm 49:4 (5, Heb.) sets out to answer. To engage in these mind-sharpening encounters with all comers was to bring one's beliefs out into the open. It implied that the truth one lived by was valid through and through, and that its writ ran everywhere; it also suggested that shared ground existed between the truly wise of any nation. Accordingly we shall come across sayings and concerns that were common property of Israelite and foreign sages; and we may notice that in 1 Kings 4:30–31 Solomon's wisdom is compared with that of the East and of Egypt, as well as that of his fellow Israelites. True, he outshone them all; but there was a basis of comparison between them. It was because his wisdom surpassed rather than by-passed theirs, that they flocked to hear him.

Wisdom's 'native wood-notes'

Incalculable as was Solomon's part in this cultural explosion, he was not starting from an intellectual void. Israel, like any other people, had its store of native wit: its sage old characters and clever young men; its sharp sayings and its more elaborate and oblique ones. A few of these happen to break surface here and there in the narratives: there are the

---

[1]See, *e.g.*, R. de Vaux, *Ancient Israel* (Darton, Longman & Todd, 1961), pp.123, 129–132.

four names in 1 Kings 4:31, from Ethan to Darda, obviously
famous in their day; there were professonal counsellors such
as Ahithophel and Hushai his rival (2 Sa. 15:12 – 17:23).
More informally, there were star performers in their own
localities: the crafty Jonadab (2 Sa. 13:3), the wise woman of
Tekoa whom we meet in 2 Samuel 14, and even a city that
was noted for its collective wisdom (Abel, 2 Sa. 20:18). An
occasional proverb flashes out: from David to Saul in 1 Samuel 24:13, on the act that reveals the man; or from Ahab to
Ben-hadad on (in our terms) counting one's chickens before
they are hatched (1 Ki. 20:11); or later on, there is the wry
joke that went the rounds in the last days of the kingdom:

> The fathers have eaten sour grapes,
> and the *children's* teeth are set on edge.
>
> Je. 31:29; Ezk. 18:2.

Or, as we might put it, '*They* ate the crab-apples, *we* get the
gripes!'

As for some other kinds of sayings, we have already
noticed Samson's verse-riddle, and it is worth pointing out
that while the answer escaped the Philistines, they seemed
familiar with the form of the puzzle. At greater length and
with a sharper point there was Jotham's fable of the trees
that sought a king (Jdg. 9:8–15) – on which Joash of Israel
would produce a devastating little variant one day about a
thistle's dreams of grandeur (2 Ch. 25:18). Again, parables
could be equally potent and polished, as is clearly shown by
Nathan's to David (2 Sa. 12:1ff.); and, as if that were not
enough, we have the woman of Tekoa spinning a parabolic
web that caught the king again (2 Sa. 14:4ff.). Later on (but
the form itself was not necessarily later) we find Ezekiel
weaving elaborate allegories in, for example, his chapters
16, 17 and 23; and before him Isaiah and Jeremiah (to name
no other prophets) had used the kind of extended illustra-
tion from daily life – in this case the arts of the farmer and
the potter (Is. 28:23ff.; Je. 18:1ff.) – with which the men of
wisdom loved to make their points. In the Psalms, too, we
recognize the sages' choice of words and tone of voice from
time to time, especially when the singer turns from addressing God to teaching or warning or encouraging his fellow
men (*e.g.*, in Pss. 1; 37; 127) or to grappling with disturbing
questions (as in Pss. 49 and 73).

In none of these cases do we have to suppose that wisdom
was a sudden or a late arrival, although certainly its growth
and its preoccupations were stimulated by outstanding

16

minds like Solomon's and by events that cried out for explanation. Certainly, too, through the growing importance of trained administrators in a society now organized as a kingdom, a learned class came to be recognized alongside those of priest and prophet, with its own distinctive style and prestige. There was a popular saying which named all three of these callings and defined their separate kinds of pronouncement:

> The law shall not perish from the priest, nor counsel from the wise, nor the word from the prophet (Je. 18:18).

But, as we have just seen, no one group had a monopoly of wisdom or of its forms of speech. Its root went deep and wide. Some of its most appetizing fruits were grown by amateurs; a few even crept over the wall from the gardens around. We shall visit these neighbours in Appendix A, pp.125ff.

The root of the matter

This brings us back to Solomon and his visitors from abroad. If some of their invasive fruits were fine, others were lethal and, to Solomon, irresistible. Increasingly he set himself to outshine his fellow potentates, marry into their dynasties and give house-room to their gods. As a king, his legacy was disastrous, his grandiose achievements miserably short-lived – for it was his words, and those of his successors, which triumphed where his actions failed. Unlike his personal example, his writings and their literary companions succeeded in combining openness with depth; a searching frankness with a tenacious underlying faith. The secret of it is expressed in the motto, 'The fear of the LORD is the beginning', or first principle, 'of wisdom'. In one form or another this truth meets us in all the wisdom books,[1] and it is this that keeps the shrewdness of Proverbs from slipping into mere self-interest, the perplexity of Job from mutiny, and the disillusion of Ecclesiastes from final despair.

But it is time to look more closely at these books themselves, and at their counterparts (if such they can be called) in other cultures.

[1]Pr. 1:7; 9:10; *cf.* Jb. 28:28; Ps. 111:10; Ec. 12:13.

2

The book of Proverbs
A life well managed

Several voices (not all Israelite) are heard here, and several styles ranging from exhortation to aphorism, from numerical sequences to an acrostic. In discussing them in chapter 3 we shall group them by their ways of speaking, but first it may be helpful to have them set out in their own order.

1 – 9   *A fatherly approach*: exhortations for the young.

10:1 – 22:16 *A plain man's approach*: Solomon's collection of sentence-sayings. Life's regularities, oddities, dangers and delights, noted, compared and evaluated.

22:17 – 24:22
and 24:23–34 *More fatherly teachings*: two groups of wise men's exhortations.

25 – 29   *More sentence-sayings*: gleanings from Solomon, compiled by Hezekiah's men.

30   *An observer's approach*: musings on the hidden Creator and on the idiosyncrasies of his creatures.

31   *A womanly approach*: a mother's home-truths (1–9); a wife's example (10–31).

Proverbs 1 – 9
A fatherly approach: exhortations for the young

To be faced abruptly with the hundreds of individual sayings that make up the final two-thirds of this book, like a great stretch of pebble beach to make one's way along,

18

would be more than daunting: it could be disorienting. What kind of wisdom, at bottom, and what kind of folly, are pictured in those terse and often throw-away remarks? What overriding motives? – self-preservation, self-respect, the common good? And is godliness only a pious afterthought, or is it basic?

The answers are already there, in the body of the book; but on their own they would take some finding, even some decoding. So we can be grateful to encounter this readable stretch of nine chapters before arriving at the 'beach' – glad not only of their smooth going as miniature essays, but also of their clear notices and signposts. Here at the outset, in 1:1–7, we are alerted to the kind of approach that awaits us in the main collection, and the kind of wisdom that will be offered us. The approach is neatly summarized in the four terms of 1:6, which the New English Bible (NEB) translates as 'proverbs . . . parables . . . sayings . . . riddles' – all of them designed not to spoon-feed the reader but to prick him into thought, whether by their vivid pictures and analogies or by the sharpness of their brevity and their teasing refusal to explain themselves. It will be very different from the preaching and the appeals that launch the book on its way in these preliminary chapters.

But it will also be different from philosophizing, at least in the sense of searching for a systematic statement of the nature of reality. True, it will encourage clear thinking (to 'understand words of insight', as 1:2 puts it), but the wisdom it speaks of is the kind that must engage the whole man: not only his power to think straight, but his management of affairs, his sensitivity to people, his character and his morals; above all (or rather, at the root of all) his relation to God. For 'the fear of the LORD' – that filial reverence which the Old Testament expounds from first to last – is not a mere beginner's step in wisdom, to be left behind, but the prerequisite of every right attitude. Only so will the world be seen the right way up, and life begin to reveal its intended pattern.

After the opening paragraph the first thing that may strike us is an unmistakable flavour of old-fashioned virtue and strong family life. In itself, the repeated expression, 'my son', need amount to no more than a teacher's fatherly way of speaking to a pupil, as in the old Egyptian instruction manuals;[1] and one must bear in mind the wide readership

[1]See Appendix A, pp.125ff.

that the author obviously has in view. But appeal will be made to the teaching and discipline of both father and mother (1:8; 6:20), and at one point the grandparents come fondly into remembrance as well (4:3). Not only in these early chapters but in every section of the book it is assumed that truth is to be learnt first at home, instilled there with firmness and affection as lessons for the mind and training for the character.

The family, of course, is not everything, even in this group of chapters. There will be other themes, especially in chapter 3 where one's neighbour and his needs, rights and influence will be the subject of short sayings (3:27ff.), and in chapter 6 where pungent remarks are aimed at the person who is imprudent (1–5), idle (6–11) or a social pest (12–19). But the home remains the place from which this teaching emanates, and whatever threatens its integrity is viewed here with profound concern.

Two such threats are given special treatment. First, in 1:10–19 (*cf.* 4:14–19), there is the fatal appeal of the gang to the restlessness of youth. We hear the heady talk of violence and loot, of an escape from tame conformity and youthful nonentity, promising a smarter prize than the 'fair garland' (9) of goodness. Yet a garland, we are reminded, is better than a noose (*cf.* 17–19), and there is nothing clever in walking into one's own trap.

Secondly there is the more subtle threat of sexual temptation. It dominates these chapters. Characteristically, it is put in vivid and dramatic terms, and the young man who is especially in mind is warned not against temptation in the abstract, but against the temptress in all her alluring actuality. She is called at one point an evil woman (6:24), but most often a stranger or outsider (using the virtually synonymous Hebrew terms *zārâ* or *nokriyyâ*) – yet her foreignness does not have to be literal. The point is that she has put herself outside the loyalties and structures of society and the laws of God, and owes her disruptiveness and much of her fascination to that intriguing fact.[1]

The portraiture is lively. Her talk drips with charm and plausibility (5:3), and she knows how to sweep a fool off his feet with a mixture of impudence and flattery, enticement and reassurance, as we learn in the compelling little drama of 7:10–21. Behind this façade, and revealed in these chap-

[1]On the suggestion that she is a cult-prostitute of Ishtar/Astarte, see pp.41f.

ters with shocking suddenness, she emerges as a character riddled with contradictions. On the one hand she has the slipperiness of the quitter and the inveterate improviser – a creature who walks out on her sworn promises to God and man (2:17), and has not a serious thought in her head ('her course turns this way and that, and what does she care?' 5:6, NEB) – while, on the other hand, towards her quarry she has the steely cunning and persistence of the predator (5:4; 7:10–12).

But if she has no scruples, her victim has no excuse. The one she stalks in chapter 7 may be young and foolish, but the real trouble is that he is unprincipled – for the fear of the LORD does not even enter his thoughts. The two of them, the huntress and the hunted in these chapters, touch the two extremes of what we now call permissiveness: its hidden ruthlessness and open fecklessness. Their unchastity is seen for what it is, stripped of its romantic colouring and traced to its bitter end.

For while the temptress has many strings to her bow, so has the teacher. He can warn us against her with the thrust of a proverb:

> Can a man carry fire in his bosom
> and his clothes not be burned?
> Or can one walk upon hot coals
> and his feet not be scorched?
>
> 6:27–28.

Or he can chill us with a glimpse of what lies behind her fair exterior: the wormwood after the initial honey; the cold steel after the oil of flattery (5:3–4); the chasm beneath the love-nest (2:18). As for the daring party thrown by Madam Folly, it turns out to be a *danse macabre*:

> He does not know that the dead are there,
> that her guests are in the depths of Sheol.
>
> 9:18.

In a different vein, using metaphor more sparingly, the teacher speaks in 5:7–14 of the dignity that a man surrenders by loose living; of perhaps the bondage of blackmail; of his scattered and haphazard brood which should have been a close-knit family; of venereal disease; of vain regrets; of well-nigh irretrievable disgrace. And if the risks of any philanderer are high, those of the adulterer may be literally deadly. 'An adulteress stalks a man's very life' (6:26), for there is no length to which jealousy and wounded pride may not drive a man (6:32–35).

Yet the teacher can balance this dark picture with its shining alternative, the bliss of faithful marriage. In a passage of rare beauty (5:15ff.) he sings of married love and fruitfulness, first in allusive metaphors of secluded wells and fountains, in contrast to the wasted springs of promiscuity ('shall your well overflow into the road, your runnels of water pour into the street?' 5:16, NEB mg.). Then, more lyrically, he bids the foolish husband look again upon his wife with a lover's wonder and total dedication:

> Find joy with the wife you married in your youth,
> fair as a hind, graceful as a fawn.
> Let hers be the company you keep,
> hers the breasts that ever fill you with delight,
> hers the love that ever holds you captive.
>
> 5:18–19, JB.

This is hardly less ardent than the poetry of the Song of Solomon, where the lover likewise compares his chaste bride to 'a garden enclosed', and rhapsodizes, as he alone may, over her bodily perfection. Yet in Proverbs it is the teacher who must do the praising, to reawaken love and to unmask its counterfeit. But his ultimate appeal is not to joy or even to the fear of disillusion. It is to the fear of Yahweh:

> For a man's ways are before the eyes of the LORD,
> and he watches all his paths.
>
> 5:21.

But alongside these direct appeals there is yet another mode in which the teacher woos us from the parody of love and from all other false delights.

The figure of Wisdom

Against the fatal charms of the whore and the adulteress (perhaps, too, of the pagan goddesses and their hierodules[1]), and indeed of folly itself in all its forms, there is presented to us the figure of Wisdom as the soul's true bride, true counsellor, true hostess, and as the very offspring of the Creator. In Proverbs 1 – 9 this figure varies with the context: seen now as an imperious preacher who will not be silenced or confined, but heard in every street (1:20ff.; 8:1ff.); then, by contrast, as one who in her reticence must be sought out and

---

[1]This is discussed in the next chapter, pp.41f.

22

waited for, as by an earnest pupil (8:34), or cherished as by a dear friend (7:4), indeed as by a husband ('Do not forsake her . . .; love her. . .; prize her . . .; embrace her . . .', 4:6, 8; *cf.* 8:17). Or again, she is Lady Bountiful, with everything to give, from riches and honour to righteousness and life itself (3:15–18; 8:18–21, 35); and her feast, like that of the gospel, is for the hungriest and the least promising. 'To him who is without sense she says, "Come, eat . . . and drink . . . . Leave . . ., and live, and walk in the way of insight" ' (9:4–6).

These exalted claims for the lady Wisdom raise the question of her actual status. Is she being presented to us as a member of the angelic hierarchy, or only as an idea personified? To me it is clear that while some of this language was destined to prepare the way for the New Testament's Christology, the portrait in its own context is personifying a concept, not describing a personality. The whole treatment is bold and flexible. This comes out particularly clearly in two successive passages in chapters 6 and 7, where God's training of us is described first in impersonal and then in personal terms, offering precisely the same benefits in each case. In 6:23–24 it is 'the commandment . . . the teaching . . . and the reproofs of discipline' which will 'preserve you from the evil woman, from the smooth tongue of the adventuress'. In 7:4–5 it is wisdom and insight, treated as one's 'sister' and 'intimate friend', which will preserve you from these same perils, described in almost identical words.

Each way of putting it has its strengths and limitations, and each complements the other. The portrait of a charming (if formidable!) confidante and guide makes godliness look quietly attractive as well as right, outshining the brassy appeal of Madam Folly (chapter 9) and of other more tangible madams. Yet wisdom, seen purely in these terms, remains a voice from without, important as this objectivity is. We need the other concept as well, whereby wisdom, learnt from the mouth of God (2:6), 'will come into your heart' (2:10) so that you *become* wise. Your mind is then guarded from within, in much the same way as that of a craftsman or an artist or a scholar, whose trained judgment arms him against what fails to ring true in his own field.

To look more closely at the two chapters, 8 and 9, which crown this great section of the book, is to find the praise of wisdom reaching a climax of eloquence and urgency. She is again personified, but her person merges with her teachings. To possess her, a prize 'better than jewels', is not to enjoy some mystical experience but to listen to truth (8:6–8), accept discipline (*mûsārî*, 10), learn prudence (5,12) and find knowledge (9,12). And while wisdom is the secret of true success in any realm (8:15–21), it is not the success of the thruster or the schemer. There is a rush of moral terms in 8:6–9, 'noble', 'right', 'truth', 'righteous', 'straight'; and in 8:13 a sharpened version of the motto-text of the book:

> The fear of the LORD is hatred of evil.
> Pride and arrogance and the way of evil
> and perverted speech I hate.

Then, as the poem takes wings in verses 22–31, wisdom is seen as the very principle of all creation, issuing from the mind of God,[1] present at every moment of his activity, and delighting supremely in the human race. While the New Testament will show that such language had depths in it which only the incarnation would bring to light, the chapter itself treats its description not as a theological excursion for the mind, but as a challenge to the will. For the passage refuses to end here. With its *'Now, my sons, . . .'* it presses for immediate response. If *this* is wisdom's status, if this was the making of us in the first place, then to turn from it is nothing less than to choose one's own unmaking. To find it, at any cost, is nothing less than life. (To which the New Testament will bring its unique and transforming information that we are now to see this lifegiver not as 'it' but as 'him': 'Christ the power of God and the wisdom of God', and to see the life-gift as eternal.[2])

Unabashed by any fear of anticlimax, chapter 9 presses home this challenge with the bold simplicity of a cartoon, sketching for us Wisdom and Folly as rival hostesses, who invite us in their very different styles to rival feasts of life or death. With that knife-edge choice, indeed with a shudder for the man who chooses wrongly, this long prelude to the anthology of terse sayings that will follow brings its series of appeals to an unforgettable conclusion.

Proverbs 10:1 – 22:16 and 25 – 29
A plain man's approach: terse sayings on the way things are

Here at last are the sayings that we recognize as proverbs:

---

[1] While discussion has tended to seize on the word in verse 22 which can be translated either 'created' or 'possessed' (lit. 'acquired'; *cf.* the repeated 'get' in 4:7), the main emphasis here is on wisdom as *begotten* ('brought forth' . . . 'brought forth', 24–25).   [2] 1 Cor. 1:24, 30; 1 Jn. 5:11–12.

short, self-contained, poured out apparently at random. Once in a while there will be a small cluster round a single theme[1] (mostly in the collection made by Hezekiah's scribes, chapters 25 – 29; seldom in 10 – 22), or sometimes a saying will spread to three or four lines[2] or even a paragraph;[3] but the standard unit is a single verse, a couplet of about six or seven Hebrew words in all (usually three strong beats answered by another three).

Even this may well have been twice the length of a typical folk-saying, for the written proverb takes the form of Hebrew poetry with its echoing second line to answer and enrich the first. Where David, for instance, quoted to Saul a single-line 'proverb of the ancients' in just three Hebrew words,

Out-of-the-wicked comes-forth wickedness,[4]

the proverbs of Solomon would have added a companion line, either to amplify it as in, *e.g.*, 21:10,

The soul of the wicked desires evil;
his neighbour finds no mercy in his eyes

or else to sharpen it with a contrast as in, *e.g.*, 12:6,

The words of the wicked lie in wait for blood,
but the mouth of the upright delivers men.

So these literary couplets are both like and unlike popular proverbs. Almost everywhere folk-wisdom is short and sharp, despite the occasional exception. In English we have a few couplets such as

You can take a horse to water,
but you can't make it drink,

yet on the whole, brevity reigns supreme with

Beggars can't be choosers;
Least said, soonest mended;
Penny wise, pound foolish;
It's a sad house where the hen crows loudest;
None so deaf as those who won't hear;
He that knows little soon repeats it

– and so on. But what the biblical proverbs lose in speed

[1]*E.g.* 10:18–21 on the use of words; 16:12–15 and 25:2–7 on kings; 26:13–16 on the sluggard; 26:20–28 on mischief-making.
[2]*E.g.* 25:20; 25:21–22; 26:18–19; 26:24–25; 27:10; 27:15–16.
[3]27:23–27 on the satisfactions of sound farming.
[4]1 Sa. 24:13.

they gain in weight, though their parentage is pretty clearly the kind of terse remark that David quoted, or that Ezekiel threw at Jerusalem: 'Like mother, like daughter' (Ezk. 16:44). By contrast, the homilies of chapters 1 – 9, and of 'the wise' in 22:17 to 24:34, and of King Lemuel's mother in 31:1–9, show a family likeness to the full-length Instructions of ancient Egypt. And while the homilies persuade and exhort us, these sentence-sayings simply state a matter and leave it at that.

Naturally they generalize, as a proverb must, and may therefore be charged with making life too tidy to be true. But nobody objects to this in secular sayings, for the very form demands a sweeping statement and looks for a hearer with his wits about him. We need no telling that a maxim like 'Many hands make light work' is not the last word on the subject, since 'Too many cooks spoil the broth'. Just so, Proverbs is not afraid to put two clashing counsels side by side in 26:4–5 (on the thankless task of answering a fool), or to balance its praise of careful planning with frank warnings elsewhere that while man proposes, God disposes. On the one hand,

> Without counsel plans go wrong,
>   but with many advisers they succeed,[1]

while on the other hand,

> Many are the plans in the mind of a man,
>   but it is the purpose of the LORD that will
>   be established.[2]

Yet when this has been said, it remains true that these sayings almost unbrokenly present the picture of merit rewarded and lapses penalized, apparently in this life.[3] A rare glimpse of the unfairness of things is seen in 13:23 (NEB),

> Untilled land might yield food enough for the poor,
>   but even that may be lost through injustice,

but it comes as the exception to the rule which neighbouring verses state in terms such as

> A righteous man eats his fill,
>   but the wicked go hungry.
>
>   13:25, NEB.

[1]15:22. [2]19:21; *cf*. 16:1,9; 20:24; 21:30–31.
[3]See, however, pp.118f.

Of course, so rosy a view of things is asking for trouble. To say that the more honestly you live and the harder you work, the better you will fare, is to state a very salutary general truth. But it may blind the dogmatically minded to the glaring exceptions to that rule, as it blinded Job's three comforters. On the other hand it may, and in fact did, help to make that glare intolerable, sharpening the problem that is thrashed out in the whole book of Job, and urgently inviting the protests and probings of Ecclesiastes. We shall revert to this point in our final chapter.

From 'platitude' to parable

If one reaction to the sentence-sayings is to think them over-confident, another may be to find a number of them platitudinous. There is some force in this, although less than we might suppose – for what may seem at first sight a mere truism may well be nothing of the sort. Is it only a tautology to say, for instance, in 12:17,

> He who speaks the truth gives honest evidence,
>   but a false witness utters deceit

or is it advising us how to judge between two rival stories, by considering the characters of those who are telling them? Is it also perhaps a warning against yes-men: that the man who will agree to say whatever suits you is really doing whatever suits *him* – and which way will he turn next time?

Even platitudes, however, if such there be, have their humble uses; for a writer can be too original. To be epigrammatic all the time may be entertaining, but it can pall; and worse, it can leave the basic truths unstated and seemingly belittled. The very things that, we feel, should go without saying may, if left unsaid, go by default. They may be self-evident to us by now, only because at some stage they were dinned into our reluctant ears with small regard for novelty.

Further, G. von Rad[1] has drawn attention to Herder's observation that to record the ways in which things regularly happen is no small step towards charting our environment and recognizing the universal laws behind the confusing cataract of events. These laws, moreover, Proverbs traces to their origin in the LORD; which gives them a sig-

---

[1]*Old Testament Theology*, I (English edition, Oliver & Boyd, 1962), pp.419ff.

nificance far beyond their utility value.

Along with this plain speaking, however, there is a wealth of imagery and comparison, and it is this that doubtless gave the proverb or parable its Hebrew name *māšāl*[1] in the first place, although it has come to include sayings and writings of many other kinds.[2]

To see a sudden likeness between two separate things, especially if the one is abstract and the other concrete, is sometimes to learn much in a moment; and this is the force of many a simile here. We may get the shock of a fierce value-judgment:

> Like a gold ring in a swine's snout
> is a beautiful woman without discretion.
>
> 11:22.

Or we may see the beauty of an unobtrusive virtue:

> Like the cold of snow in the time of harvest
> is a faithful messenger to those who send him,
> he refreshes the spirit of his masters.
>
> 25:13.

Or realize the lingering influence of the gossip we enjoy:

> The words of a whisperer are like delicious morsels;
> they go down into the inner parts of the body.
>
> 26:22.

Or the power of quiet persistence:

> With patience a ruler may be persuaded,
> and a soft tongue will break a bone.
>
> 25:15.

But some of these comparisons hold more than meets the eye. Below the surface there may lurk a parable. Is it only gastronomic sense that warns us in 25:16,

> If you have found honey, eat only enough for you,
> lest you be sated with it and vomit it,

---

[1] *I.e.*, from the root *mšl*, to be like. Another root *mšl* means to rule; hence some interpret the *māšāl* as a 'potent saying'. But potency is far more characteristic of prophetic oracles or priestly blessings, which help to bring their own fulfilment, than of wisdom sayings which invite reflection.

[2] *E.g.* discourses (Pr. 1 – 9); predictions (Nu. 23:7); teachings (Pss. 49:4 [5, Heb.]; 78:2); allegories (Ezk. 17:2); witticisms (Ezk. 18:2); taunts (Is. 14:4); bywords (Je. 24:9).

or is it a warning against the hedonism which ends only in ennui or ignominy? Is it simply social prudence that warns us in 25:6–7 not to be pushing?

> For it is better to be told, "Come up here,"
> than to be put lower in the presence of the prince.

Our Lord saw more in it than that (Lk. 14:7–11). And in Proverbs 25:4–5 a saying ostensibly about good craftsmanship is applied quite explicitly to moral and political affairs:

> Take away the dross from the silver,
> and the smith has material for a vessel;
> take away the wicked from the presence of the king,
> and his throne will be established in righteousness.

But comparison has a further use. It may point out differences as well as likenesses, and so evaluate one thing by reference to another. Sometimes the comparison will be explicit, in the many sayings which begin with the word 'Better' (of which more anon), but sometimes only implicit. Proverbs gets us to compare the 'now' of an act with its 'afterwards'. We watch the wine sparkling in the cup, but face what follows when it is loved too much (23:29–35). We look at easy money, but notice that what lightly comes lightly goes (13:11). Or at illicit sex in the light of what awaits it 'in the end' (5:4).[1] More cheerfully, we compare the irksomeness of accepting good advice with the blessings it will bring one day (19:20). And when it seems too costly to be godly, we are helped to see the picture as a whole:

> Surely there is a future,
> and your hope will not be cut off.
>
> 23:18.

The criteria: moral or mercenary?

The encouragement to look ahead or carefully around can easily become too calculating – and there are moments when Proverbs runs the risk of such a charge. It has no taste for wild adventures, and no disdain for legitimate self-interest:

---

[1]The word for 'afterwards' or 'in the end', *etc.*, variously translated, will repay study, at 5:4,11; 14:12–13; 16:25; 19:20; 20:21; 23:18, 32; 24:14, 20; 25:8; 29:21.

> A shrewd man sees trouble coming and lies low;
> the simple walk into it and pay the penalty.
>
> 27:12, NEB.

> A man who is kind benefits himself,
> but a cruel man hurts himself.
>
> 11:17.

Sometimes there is even a studied neutrality – or so it may seem – over some dubious practice which is recorded without comment:

> A gift in secret averts anger;
> and a bribe in the bosom, strong wrath.
>
> 21:14 (yet see 15:27).

But a teacher, especially one who deals in aphorisms and vignettes, does not have to moralize incessantly. It is enough to make his standpoint clear, and let the reader judge for himself what chimes or jars with it.

That standpoint is as confessedly orthodox in these sections of the book as in chapters 1 – 9, as a glance at 16:1–9 in particular will confirm – supported by the more sporadic referring of matters back to the LORD in every chapter.[1] So, however shrewdly we are urged to calculate, it is not material profit or loss, but moral values and the LORD's approval, which have the last word here. Some things are said to be better than others because of their convenience, but others are just 'better', come what may. It is better to be poor and honest than rich and crooked (28:6); better to be numbered with the humble than to hobnob with the proud (16:19); better to rule one's spirit than even to capture a city (16:32).[2] And lest we should still interpret these comparisons as no more than different shades of grey, they are reinforced with black-and-white antitheses between the wicked and the righteous, the evil and the upright, especially in the opening chapters of this part of the book (*i.e.* 10ff.).

Indeed, to the scandal of the sophisticated, one of the

---

[1]The significance of this can be challenged if one adopts the hypothesis that sayings about the LORD are secondary or tertiary additions; but there is no hard evidence for this, either in these chapters or in 1 – 9. See further, pp.47ff.

[2]The use of 'Better' as a teaching device is equally prominent in Ecclesiastes (but often paradoxically there, to challenge easy assumptions: *e.g.* Ec. 7:1ff.). In Proverbs, it is found at 3:14; 8:11, 19; 12:9; 15:16–17; 19:1, 22; 21:9, 19; 22:1; 25:7, 24; 27:5, 10; 28:6.

hallmarks of this wisdom teaching is the insistence that between right and wrong there is no middle way. Somewhere between the two – that is, between the fear of the LORD and any alternative – there may seem to be a reasonable compromise, 'a way which seems right to a man'; but Proverbs, like Psalm 1 or the Sermon on the Mount (*e.g.* Mt.7:13ff.), will have none of it. 'Its end is the way to death' (14:12).

Yet all this is done with a light touch and with a keen eye for the finer points of the way we treat each other. The tactless friend who 'sings songs to a heavy heart' or outstays his welcome or gets you up too early;[1] the practical joker;[2] the idler and his preposterous excuses;[3] the wrongheaded and the pigheaded;[4] the gossip;[5] – all these are almost as disastrous as the downright wicked, and their opposites are a joy to God and man. But we learn our lessons from them better by a flash of wit than by a roll of sermonic thunder. And by finding room for these apparent trivialities (which are, after all, the very stuff of everyday encounters) Proverbs claims the whole of life for wisdom, and the whole range of wisdom for God.

Proverbs 22:17 – 24:34
Another fatherly approach: 'Words of Wise Men'

Between the two collections of Solomon's sentence-sayings[6] we have a refreshing change of style and source, with its own earnest little introduction (22:17–19) and a short supplement in 24:23ff.

The tone is warm and personal, mostly appealing to us directly with its 'don'ts' and occasional 'do's', rather than simply stating a thing with the cool economy of a typical proverb.[7] Many of its themes are those that meet us in the other collections – mercy to the poor; wise friendships; financial prudence; firmness with children; hard work; sexual purity; and so on – but there are special emphases as well, and some unforgettable descriptions. Two of the special themes are, first, that of quiet trust instead of fretfulness (23:17–18; 24:19ff.), along the lines which are developed at length in Psalm 37; and secondly, the generous compassion

---

[1]Pr. 25:20, 17; 27:14.   [2]26:18–19.   [3]*E.g.* 26:13–16.
[4]*E.g.* 29:9, 1.   [5]26:20ff.
[6]*I.e.* between those of 10:1 – 22:16 and those collected by Hezekiah's scholars, chapters 25 – 29.   [7]But see 24:3–9, 23–26.

which will go beyond the usual bounds, to embrace strangers and enemies (24:11–12, 17, 29). As for the descriptive sketches, there are little masterpieces on the social climber (23:1–8), the drinker (23:29–35) and the drifter (24:30–34).

Like chapters 1 – 9, and 31:1–9, these 'words of wise men' are nearer to the style of teaching-manuals that to nuggets of folk wisdom; and in 22:20 we have what now seems to be a deliberate reference to their particular prototype, in the words, 'Have I not written for you thirty sayings . . .?' If 'thirty sayings' is the right translation,[1] it almost certainly invites comparison with the currently well-known Instruction of Amenemope, which not only has many themes in common with this set of sayings, but also addresses the reader with 'See thou these thirty chapters . . .'.[2] In other words, here (it seems) is an Israelite counterpart to that Egyptian classic, in much the same way that Psalm 104 rewrites and transcends Ikhnaten's Hymn to the Sun, or that Psalm 92:9 claims for the true God what an Ugaritic poem had claimed for Baal.

A further note on chapters 25 – 29

We have already sampled these extra sayings of Solomon along with those of chapters 10 – 22; but a few remaining points call for a mention in passing.

First, on a practical note, one is less likely to get lost here than in the main collection, since Hezekiah's scribes (25:1) had evidently an eye for proverbs that could be grouped together. Here are little clusters on such subjects as kings (25:2–7), fools (26:1–12, mostly), sluggards (26:13–16) and mischief-makers (26:17–28), while chapters 25 and 27 contain a memorable sprinkling of sayings, grave and gay, on relationships with friends and neighbours.

Secondly, as already observed, a few of these proverbs run to an extra line, or to a second or third verse (*e.g.* 25:13, 20; 25:8–10, 21–22; 26:24–26), and in one case to a short poem (27:23–27, in praise of the outdoor life).

Thirdly, there is a marked emphasis, especially in chapters 28 and 29, on rulers[3] and on those who set the tone of a

---

[1]The Hebrew word has been vocalized in various ways, as, *e.g.*, NIV mg. indicates. For details, see any recent commentary.

[2]Text in *ANET*, pp.421–424. The words quoted above introduce the final 'chapter', p.424b. I discuss this further on pp.44f., below.

[3]Not only 25:2–7, as noted above, but 25:15; 27:24; 28:15–16; 29:2, 4, 12, 14, 26.

society. For example,

> Like a muddied spring or a polluted fountain
> is a righteous man who gives way before the wicked.
>
> 25:26.

> When a land transgresses
> it has many rulers;
> but with men of understanding and knowledge
> its stability will long continue.
>
> 28:2.

> Scoffers set a city aflame,
> but wise men turn away wrath.
>
> 29:8.

> Where there is no prophecy the people cast off restraint,
> but blessed is he who keeps the law.
>
> 29:18.

All in all, some of the brightest gems of the whole book are in this section.

Proverbs 30
An observer's approach: musings on the Creator and on the ways of his creatures

Here is a fresh voice and a fresh approach; very probably that of an Ishmaelite convert from northern Arabia.[1]

It is remarkable first for Agur's impassioned disclaimer of any ability to think true thoughts of God (1–4) except by revelation (4–5); or even to be loyal to him except by (in our terms) his grace and providence (7–9). Here we may intercept an ironic glance from him at his self-assured and learned colleagues, to whom theology seems child's play, and God an open book (2–3). There is a strong echo of the humbling of Job in verse 4; and the use of the term Eloah for God in verse 5 is another link with that part of Scripture and with its setting among 'the people of the east' (Jb. 1:3).

(In passing, we should mention that some scholars allow only verses 1–3 or 1–4 to Agur, thereby reducing him to a

---

[1]Taking Massa to mean here and in 31:1 the clan of that name (Gn. 25:14), rather than 'prophetic oracle' (AV, RV). Although this entails a small emendation (*e.g. mmś'*, 'from Massa', for the existing *mś'*), it gains some probability from the non-Israelite king of 31:1, where 'king of Massa' needs no emendation.

voice of total scepticism. The grounds for this, which are in my view quite inadequate, are discussed in chapter 3, pp.52f.)

Already in this heartfelt opening, with its plea, 'two things I ask of thee', there is a foretaste of the *numerical sayings* which give the chapter its special flavour. Most of them, but not all,[1] have a built-in crescendo in the formula, 'Three things . . ., (yea) four . . .'. This is striking and intriguing, both in form and content; but the form is not uncommon either in Scripture or in neighbouring literature.[2] Proverbs itself has another example in 6:16–19 ('six . . ., seven . . .'; *cf.* the 'six troubles . . ., seven . . .' of Jb. 5:19), and Amos opens with nearly two chapters of oracles which say 'For three transgressions . . ., and for four . . .'. This gives the rhythm of poetry to a saying, with its echoing beat; and it adds an extra weight to the final figure, or else perhaps a hint that the list could be extended.

As for the content and point of the sayings here, I doubt if we should try to find a single answer. Their glory is in their variety and their elusiveness. At one moment they deliver a straight moral punch, as in verses 11–14 (perhaps with a build-up from the young horrors of verse 11 to the monsters of 14 – yet perhaps, more subtly, with a dig at the self-satisfied poseurs of the two middle verses, grouped as they are with such outrageous bedfellows). At another moment a barbed shaft or a tiny set of parables may lurk beneath the surface. Which of us, dissatisfied with what we have, would not blush to find ourselves included with the horseleech (15) in our appetite for more, along with its companions of verse 16, whether pathetic, parched or menacing, which never say 'Enough'? Who can fail to take heart from the initiative of the four things small but wise (24–28)?

But not all have a moral to convey. Interspersed with some of the sharpest of short sayings[3] there are what appear to be simply a collector's gallery of choice exhibits, noticed with an artist's eye, and grouped to set off one another's styles and characters. So we experience his fascination with the four things 'too wonderful' for him, with his four in-

---

[1] Verses 11–14 dispense with an introduction; and verses 24–28 simply speak of 'four things'.

[2] *Cf., e.g.,* the Ugaritic Baal Epic: 'Two banquets Baal hates, Three the Rider of the clouds . . .' (*ANET*, p.132b). For a fuller study of this form, see G. Sauer, *Die Sprüche Agurs* (*BWANT* 84, 1963); W. M. W. Roth, *Numerical Sayings in the OT* (*VTS* 13, 1965).

[3] *I.e.* verses 10, 17, 20 (on the hardened sinner), 32–33.

sufferable types, and with his four majestic movers (but is there a gentle hint there, in 29–31, of the thin line between the stately and the strutting, in the choice of at least one of the king's fellow striders?):

> . . . the lion, which is mightiest among beasts
> and does not turn back before any;
> the strutting cock, the he-goat,
> and a king striding before his people.

If any chapter in the Bible could be called an artist's or journalist's exemplar, surely it should be this. For it not only encourages a lively interest in our fellow beings of all shapes and sizes, but combines this insatiable curiosity with, on the one hand, a deep humility in face of mystery, and on the other hand, a clear insistence on the values that have been revealed to us. If Agur's opening remarks prepare us for a childlike attitude, the progress of the chapter displays not only childlike wonder but the devastating candour of one who – like the infant in the story of the Emperor's New Clothes – observes exactly what is there, and says exactly what he sees.

Proverbs 31
A womanly approach: a mother's home-truths (1–9) and a wife's example (10–31)

Although the Septuagint gives the last word to only one of these two decisive women,[1] the placing of this double challenge to form the book's conclusion (in the Hebrew Bible, as in our own versions) leaves us with a lively presentation of the two main elements in Proverbs: instruction and observation. The fatherly counsels of chapters 1 – 9 and 22:17 – 24:34 now crackle with a mother's vehemence in verses 1–9, while the cooler maxims of the body of the book take living shape in the final poem, the portrait of the exemplary wife.

The former passage, the words of King Lemuel's mother, comes nearest of all the Instructions to the Egyptian examples, in being addressed to a ruler about his responsibilities. At the same time, its passionate reproaches in verses 2–4 ('What, my son?') give it the stamp of a personal, first-hand appeal to an actual son; and his transmission of the message tells its own story of his due acceptance of these powerful rebukes.

[1] LXX places 30:1 – 31:9 at the end of chapter 24.

In the second passage, that 'A to Z' of wifely virtues (for verses 10–31 are an alphabetic acrostic), we meet many of the qualities that have coloured the whole book. Here is a woman who leaves nothing to chance; who uses her organizing ability, her skilful hands, her business sense and every minute of her time, to create a ménage where nothing is second-rate or insecure, where wisdom and faithfulness abound; where help is at hand for the hard-pressed and where family bonds are affectionate and strong. At the root of it all, we are told, is the fear of the LORD. It is the picture of a godliness that is severely practical, of values that are sound and humane, and of a success that has been most diligently earned.

True, the paragon who has achieved all this is unusually gifted and well placed. Proverbs itself – to say nothing of Job and Ecclesiastes – admits elsewhere that life is seldom as unclouded or predictable as this. But here are the disciplined qualities and habits that make for stability and that work with the grain in God's world. Only a fool would undervalue them.

Stability is not everything. There is a time for change; there is danger in tranquillity, and there is room in God's will for the wholly unexpected and unexplained. The other Wisdom books will take ample care of these. But we do not have to be paralysed by such uncertainties, or despise the built-in regularities which make nine-tenths of life manageable and quietly rewarding. It is this large area which Proverbs insists that we take seriously, sensibly, confidently and from the hand of God.

3

Proverbs and modern study

Critical study of Proverbs has recently paid growing attention to the sayings and instruction manuals of the ancient Near East – a pursuit which the author of 1 Kings would presumably have welcomed in view of his comparison of Solomon's wisdom with that of 'all the people of the east, and all the wisdom of Egypt'.[1] This interest in the culture of Israel's nearer neighbours, as a factor to be reckoned with throughout her history, has replaced an earlier critical preoccupation with the wisdom of Greece in this area: an influence which Israel was to encounter in any depth only in the last two or three centuries before Christ.

A second tool of study has been form-criticism, which, for all its limitations, offers a more objective way of 'placing' the types of material in the book than did the search for clues from history and from the estimated evolution of Israel's theology. It can be misapplied, however, as it was when its data were interpreted to conform with Gunkel's theory that wisdom sayings developed from the short and secular to the long and lofty. Accordingly the material in Proverbs was generally dated (until a few decades ago) by the length and content of its units, assuming reasonably enough that its two-line sayings were a literary elaboration of the pithy, one-line type of folk-saying found elsewhere in the Old Testament,[2] but going on to plot an imagined progress within the book from its two-liners to its four-liners and upwards, and from bare statements to moralistic exhorta-

[1] 1 Ki. 4:30 (5:10, Heb.)
[2] See above, pp.25f. Note, incidentally, that the explicitly ancient saying quoted in 1 Sa. 24:13 was already concerned with morality and its springs, *contra* Gunkel.

tions. The possibility that aphorisms and exhortations might be two distinct species, rather than two stages in a linear development, was slow to win any recognition.

This point will come up a little more fully in the next section, which looks at some changing views of Proverbs 1 – 9 and its companion pieces. The rest of the chapter will then take samples of some critical studies of the other collections in Proverbs.

Fatherly[1] instructions: wisdom in the imperative mood
a. Proverbs 1 – 9; b. Proverbs 22:17 – 24:34; c. Proverbs 31:1–9

a. Proverbs 1 – 9

The opening words, 'The proverbs of Solomon . . .', may be viewed as introducing either chapters 1 – 9 themselves or (as I would think) the main material in the book – a title to be picked up again at 10:1[2] after these chapters have duly prepared the reader 'to understand a proverb and a figure, the words of the wise and their riddles' (1:6) in the right spirit of godly humility (1:7).

In the early years of this century these chapters were usually assigned to approximately the third century BC, on the grounds that their fatherly appeal to reason was an approach developed after the imperious voice of prophecy had fallen silent; that their concepts (especially the personification of Wisdom) were indebted to Greek thought;[3] or Gunkel-wise, that their sustained and pious discourse was the product of a long evolution of the wisdom saying. Since

[1]'Fatherly' must be stretched to include 'motherly' (*e.g.* 1:8; 6:20; and especially 31:1–9), also the voice of personified Wisdom (1:20ff.; 8:1ff.; 9:1ff.) and of Wise Men (22:17; 24:23).

[2]Note that 10:1, unlike 25:1, does not use the expression, '*These also* are proverbs of Solomon', as though introducing a second Solomonic collection.

[3]*E.g.* C. H. Toy (*Proverbs*, *ICC*, 1899) reckoned that 'in all its parts' (p.vi) Proverbs identified virtue with knowledge, and therefore belonged to the Greek period after Alexander (p.xxii). This late date was confirmed for him by the book's tacit assumption of monotheism and monogamy, by its non-mention of such terms as 'Israel', 'temple', 'priest', 'prophet', and by its emphasis on the sage's torah rather than that of Yahweh. Socially, its warnings against gossip, greed, violence and unchastity reflected, to his mind, urban rather than rural temptations; and even the references to kings seemed to him closer to court life in Josephus than to that of the pre-exilic monarchy (pp.xx–xxii).

the 1950s, however, while many scholars continue to see these chapters as probably the latest in the book, there has been fresh thinking about their provenance. For a start, the wise are no longer seen as late-comers in Israel but as a distinct voice – and perhaps a professional class of court scribes and counsellors[1] – from almost the start of the monarchy. As for the supposed signs of Greek influence, it is now generally agreed that the true milieu of Israelite wisdom was both nearer and older, namely the ancient orient. In 1955 W. F. Albright argued with characteristic vigour that we should look to Israel's Canaanite and Phoenician neighbours, not only for linguistic light on Proverbs (as M. J. Dahood would eagerly confirm[2]) but for echoes of their mythology. 'Proverbs teems with isolated Canaanitisms', Albright claimed;[3] and not only so, but its Wisdom cosmogony in Proverbs 8:22ff. was 'full of obvious Canaanite reminiscences'.[4] (For further views on the literary background to the personified Wisdom, see below, pp.41ff.) Indeed Albright's conclusion on the date of Proverbs was 'that its entire content is probably pre-exilic' – although much of it, in his view, would have been still 'handed down orally until the fifth century BC'.[5]

But while Albright may have overpressed his Canaanite case,[6] he had good grounds for his protest against 'the evolutionary strait jacket' (p.4) which had made it a foregone conclusion that homilies were late and aphorisms early. For it has now been shown beyond reasonable doubt that the literary prototype of such teachings as Proverbs 1 – 9, and the 'words of the wise' and of King Lemuel's mother (22:17 – 24:34, and 31:1–9), was not the spoken proverb but the

---

[1]*Cf., e.g.,* David's secretary and counsellors in 2 Sa. 8:17; 15:31ff.; 16:20ff.; and the references to Israelite and foreign politicians as 'wise men' in, *e.g.,* Is. 19:11–12; 29:14. For the view of the wise as a professional class see Crenshaw, *Old Testament Wisdom,* pp. 28f. Against, see R. N. Whybray, *The Intellectual Tradition in the Old Testament (BZAW* 135, 1974), esp. pp. 30, 54, 70. Whybray suggests that the well-known saying in Je. 18:18 may mean merely that there are three kinds of people who never stop talking! (*ibid.,* p. 30).

[2]M. J. Dahood, *Proverbs and Northwest Semitic Philology* (Rome, 1963).

[3]'Canaanite-Phoenician Sources in Hebrew Wisdom', *VTS* 3, 1955, p.9.

[4]*Ibid.,* pp. 7f. For criticism of some of Albright's assertions see W. McKane, *Proverbs,* pp. 354–356; R. N. Whybray, *Wisdom in Proverbs,* pp.83ff.

[5]*Ibid.,* p.13.

[6]*E.g.,* Whybray finds only one convincing Canaanitism in Pr. 8 – 9: *viz.* the form *qrt,* 'city', instead of the more common Heb. *qryh.* (*op. cit.,* p.84, n.3).

written Instruction, of which many examples survive, especially from Egypt. Some extracts from these training texts for administrators are given in Appendix A, below (pp.125ff.). Here was a long-standing and international form of teaching which, like these sections of Proverbs, addressed the reader as 'my son', setting him a high ethical and professional standard, expounded in straight discourse rather than disconnected aphorisms, and with exhortations rather than bare statements. Solomon's close links with Egypt, and his need to train a new class of administrators, could well have drawn his attention to such teaching aids (*cf.* his use of Hiram's experts, 1 Ki. 7:13; 9:27) – although Proverbs makes something new of the form, instructing not professionals (apart from King Lemuel) but all comers, and relating all wisdom to its true source, the LORD.

McKane has summed up the implications of this diagnosis with the comment: 'The Instruction is a separate genre from the wisdom sentence, and the form-critical argument for the lateness of these sections of the book of Proverbs, involving as it does the assumption that their basic formal unit is the wisdom sentence, falls to the ground.'[1]

Nevertheless the evolutionary quest finds other outlets. In 1965 R. N. Whybray published his *Wisdom in Proverbs*,[2] drawing attention to the Egyptian Instructions not simply as a literary model for Proverbs 1 – 9 but as the source of its ideology in the first place. The first draft of each of the 'ten discourses' in this section (he argued) reflected the Egyptian concepts of order (*ma'at*), of the quiet man as against the hot and passionate one, of a rather distant divinity, and of the sufficiency of human reason. This material suffered two successive revisions to bring it to the form in which we know it. 'Group One' additions identified the teacher's instructions with a quality called 'wisdom', sometimes personified; then 'Group Two' additions made this wisdom divine in origin. By this gradual process the tension was eased between Word and Wisdom, the prophet and the sage; *i.e.* between the old concept of Yahweh's all-pervading initiative to which man responds purely as an obedient listener, and that of a divinely wise world-order which confronts him in his capacity as a thinker.

Whybray's scheme, however, rests on debatable opinions and, more seriously, on a mutilated text. His opinion, for instance, that the expression 'my torah' (*e.g.* 3:1; 4:2) set the

[1]*Proverbs*, p.7.   [2]*Studies in Biblical Theology* 45 (SCM Press).

human teacher in rivalry with *the* torah, does not survive comparison with the similar pair of New Testament terms, 'my gospel' and 'the gospel'; and in any case the supposed conflict arises only when the expression is lifted from its godly context. Given that liberty one can prove anything. Again, the hard words of the Prophets against the Wise (to which Whybray appeals) were directed at those who pitted their wits against God, not at seekers after the wisdom that Solomon sought. The prophets had equally hard words for their own opinionated colleagues. As for his rearrangement of the text to yield its three stages, its severity is illustrated by his treatment of the apparently seamless chapter 2, which is reduced, for its first draft, from twenty-two verses to six (1,9,16–19) to correspond with 5:1–6 and to avoid its 'wearisome repetitions'. But what is wearisome to one man or one age may be high eloquence to another. The only control on the excisions (apart, it seems, from the circular consideration that they support the hypothesis) is the question whether or not they disrupt the flow of a given passage; but the generous (or 'wearisome') style of writing allows too much play for this control to be reliable. One has to conclude that the valuable point made by Whybray in recognizing the literary affinity between these chapters and the Egyptian teachings has been greatly overplayed by him.

The figure of Wisdom in Proverbs 1 – 9

Among the 'Canaanitisms' which Albright claimed to find in Proverbs 8 and 9 was the form *ḥokmôt* for 'wisdom' in 9:1 (also found at 1:20; 24:7; ?14:1), a form which pointed in his view to a Phoenician background, perhaps a goddess, for this figure.[1] From another angle, Boström had already suggested a Palestinian or Near Eastern milieu for chapters 1 – 9 by his argument that the whole section was a counterblast to the influence of Ishtar/Astarte and her cult-prostitutes, the latter being implied by the 'foreign woman' of 2:16, *etc.*[2] The figure of Wisdom was therefore, in his view, largely

---

[1]*Art. cit.*, *VTS* 3, pp. 8f. The form, however, can be interpreted as a plural of fullness or (BDB) emphatic abstraction.

[2]Boström (likewise Albright) adopts the LXX of 7:6–7, where it is the woman, not the narrator, who is looking out (*parakyptousa*) of the window, like *Aphroditē parakyptousa* and like the goddess or harlot depicted on various Phoenician ivories. See Albright, *art. cit.*, p.10; N. G. Boström, *Proverbiastudien* (Lund, 1934), pp. 120ff., discussed in H. Ringgren, *Word and Wisdom*, pp. 133ff.

modelled on that of the love-goddess to whom she stood in contrast as she offered love, not lust; truth, not flattery; and life instead of disillusion and death. These cultic implications, however, may be thought more ingenious that self-evident, since nothing in the text (not even 7:14, seen in context) makes the temptress necessarily a cult-servant;[1] nor is the personified Wisdom presented as the mere counterpart or response to a prior rival. In these passages she is always the first on the scene, and it is Madam Folly or the seductress who is then introduced as the negative response to her; indeed as her caricature, as in chapter 9.[2] Wisdom's precedence is absolute ('at the beginning . . .', 8:22) and her relevance universal (8:1–21).

An alternative cultural background for the personified Wisdom has been sought in the pantheons of Israel's neighbours – for polytheism has a natural bent towards turning the attributes of a high god into secondary gods or goddesses. H. Ringgren's *Word and Wisdom* surveys these deifications in Egyptian, Sumero-Accadian, West-Semitic and Pre-Islamic Arabian religions, along with a study of quasi-personal language about Wisdom, Word, Righteousness, *etc.*, in the Old Testament and in later Judaism. Among his conclusions he pointed out the crucial distinction that 'in Israelite religion and in Islam the strict monotheistic belief did not allow the hypostases to become real deities. In other religions, where this obstacle is not extant, nothing prevents the creation of new gods in this way'.[3]

Confining herself to one of these neighbouring religions, Christa Kayatz[4] draws attention to the various Egyptian tomb-texts in which a secondary deity, sponsoring the deceased, will claim high rank and high antiquity in language not unlike that of Wisdom in Proverbs 8:22ff. Thus the god Hike (magic) proclaims his ancient origin ('before there existed two things in the land'), his membership of the

---

[1]The woman's talk of sacrifices and vows just completed (7:14), and of her husband's absence till the next full moon (7:20), is construed by both Boström (*op. cit.*, pp. 107ff., 123ff.) and Ringgren (*op. cit.*, p. 136) to imply that her invitation is to an act of *cultic* fornication. This goes well beyond the evidence.

[2]Against the flow of chapter 9 (where Wisdom's feast precedes its parody) Boström (*op. cit.*, p.160), supported by McKane (*ad loc.*), regards the opening scene as secondary to that of the seductress, not vice versa.

[3]*Word and Wisdom*, p.192. Ringgren uses the word 'hypostasis' in the sense of 'a quasi-personification of certain attributes proper to God . . .'. (*ibid.*, p.8).

[4]*Studien zu Proverbien 1 – 9* (Neukirchener Verlag, 1966).

divine hierarchy, and his function in the world as 'guardian of all that the one Lord commanded'. The air god Shu claims that he is 'life', and is the first-born of the creator Atum. Isis, speaking as the 'beloved daughter' of her divine father, and endued with his knowledge, gives the invitation, 'Come to me, come to me: see, my mouth has life.' Even the god-king Rameses II can speak in similar vein. A near approach to celebrating Wisdom in such terms comes in another funerary text in which Atum's daughter Tefnut, the goddess of moisture, is called *ma'at* ('order') and described as a beloved child who (together with her brother Shu) was brought forth 'before I had founded my place . . ., before I had created Nut (the sky-goddess) . . ., before the first bodily existence was created . . .' – and so on, in terms which may remind us of the series of 'befores' in our poem. But *ma'at* is nearer to 'order' or 'sound practice' than to 'wisdom'; and as Kayatz points out,[1] it confers life not only on men but on the gods themselves.

The resemblances in these passages to Proverbs 8:22ff. are scattered (it should be remembered) among different speakers, and are coloured with magical and polytheistic ideas which are wholly foreign to Proverbs. Yet it is plausible to view these gropings as possible stimuli spurring the biblical writer to put such poetry and concepts to truer use. In Kayatz's opinion the authors of Proverbs 1 – 9 were literary theologians standing firmly in the Israelite tradition, but having access also to non-Israelite (*i.e.* Egyptian) forms and concepts in which to express their teachings. All this, for her, points to the 'Solomonic Enlightenment' as the most likely provenance of this group of chapters, as also of 10 – 29.[2]

With much the same standpoint, K. A. Kitchen's article, 'Some Egyptian Background to the Old Testament',[3] had pointed out that 'personification of qualities, attributes and objects formed part of the common intellectual heritage of the Ancient Orient, of the Bible lands themselves, from as early as the 3rd and 2nd millennia BC'. He drew attention, among many examples, to the Egyptian Hu and Sia ('Authoritative Utterance' and 'Understanding'), to the Mesopotamian Uznu and Khasisu ('Hearing' and 'Intelligence') and to similar personifications in Hurrian, Hittite and Ugaritic texts.

---

[1]*Ibid*, p.97.   [2]*Ibid.*, pp. 135f.
[3]*Tyndale House Bulletin* 5–6 (1960), pp.4ff.

'In personifying Wisdom, *c*.950 BC,' Kitchen concluded, Solomon 'would be using for the expression of divine truths a figure of mind and speech very appropriate in a world where personification of concepts like wisdom . . . had been familiar over wide areas of the Ancient East for well over a millennium before'.[1]

b. Words of the Wise
Proverbs 22:17 – 24:22 (plus 24:23–34)

This series of exhortations is reminiscent not only of Instruction literature in general, but of the 'thirty chapters' of Amenemope[2] in particular (*cf.* the mention of 'thirty sayings' in most modern versions of Pr. 22:20).[3] Ever since this work was published by Wallis Budge in 1923 it has been the consensus of scholars that Proverbs has drawn upon it for its 'Words of the Wise' – although a few voices have suggested an opposite direction of flow, or else a common source or a common stock of wisdom for both.

Some points to bear in mind about this are: (a) that Amenemope's Instruction was evidently composed before the time of Solomon (to judge by some early extant fragments of copies made from it: *e.g.* the Cairo ostracon);[4] (b) that Proverbs here appears to mention and adopt a scheme of some thirty sections[5], showing distinct resemblances to much of Amenemope's material, though not to its order. But (c)

---

[1]*Ibid.*, p.6. *Cf.* his *Ancient Orient and Old Testament* (Tyndale Press, 1966), pp.126f.

[2]For extracts and notes see *ANET*, pp. 421–424; *DOTT*, pp.172–186. For a thorough discussion see J. Ruffle, 'The Teaching of Amenemope and its Connection with the Book of Proverbs', *Tyn.B* 28 (1977), pp. 29–68.

[3]This accepts the Massoretes' emendation of *šlšwm* ('the third day' – a term found elsewhere only in the *composite* expression 'from yesterday and the third day', an idiom for 'hitherto') to read *šlšym*. This can be vocalized as the numeral 'thirty', but the Massoretes vocalized it somewhat improbably as 'officers' or 'nobles' (whence, precariously, AV, RV, 'excellent things'). Before the Amenemope text came to light, commentators mostly confessed themselves baffled by this word.

[4]Albright suggests for Amenemope the 12th century BC (*VTS* 3, p.13), J. M. Plumley *c*.1300 BC (*DOTT*, p.174); J. Ruffle before 1000 BC, perhaps as early as the 18th Dynasty, which ended *c*.1310 (Ruffle, *art. cit.*, pp.33f.). Solomon reigned from *c*.960.

[5]The GNB actually enumerates these, following McKane's analysis. Other versions and scholars differ slightly in the implied number and division of the constituent paragraphs, and some distrust the attempt to arrive at an exact thirty (*e.g.* A. Barucq, *Le Livre des Proverbes* (Gabalda, Paris, 1964), p.175).

several alleged borrowings require textual emendations;[1] (d) others could be attributed to the shared interests of a wide variety of moralists.[2] In all, it seems highly probable that this section of Proverbs knows and uses Amenemope, but sits loose to it: choosing its own order, its own emphases and its own range of subjects.

c. The words of King Lemuel's mother
Proverbs 31:1–9

This again is a direct address, in the imperative mood. Its vocational emphasis (on kingship, not on general morality) brings it especially close to the pattern of extra-biblical Instructions, since these were addressed to budding administrators, including (in the case of Amenemhet and Merikare) future kings. So, while other hortatory instructions in Proverbs point out the universal perils of loose living (*e.g.* Pr.5 on promiscuous sex; 23:29ff. on drunkenness), and the universal duty of compassion (*e.g.* 24:11–12), this one puts them in the special context of power and the heightened obligations which it brings. It spells out the principle of Luke 12:48 ('much given . . . much required') with maternal outspokenness!

Short sayings:
wisdom in the indicative mood
Proverbs 10:1 – 22:16, and chapters 25 – 29

In the present century a great store of ancient Near Eastern sentence-sayings has come to light, from Sumerian proverbs to Egyptian, and from about the time of Abraham[3] to well beyond that of Ezra and Nehemiah.[4] In form, even the earliest of them show literary artistry and variety: for example, E. I. Gordon noted that out of some 300 ancient Sumerian proverbs which are well enough preserved to show their structure, about 130 could be classified by the type of parallelism which they exhibited: *i.e.* some 54 in

[1]See my *Proverbs*, p. 23, n.1.   [2]See J. Ruffle, *art. cit.*, esp. pp. 62–68.
[3]See E. I. Gordon, *Sumerian Proverbs* (University of Pennsylvania, 1959).
[4]*The Instructions of Onchsheshonqy*, edited by S. R. K. Glanville (British Museum, 1955), are dated by Glanville to the 5th century BC. The *Papyrus Insinger*, or 'Demotic Wisdom Book', appears to belong to the Egypt of late Persian or early Ptolemaic times, *i.e.* 4th to 3rd centuries BC.

antithetic, 51 in synonymous parallelism, together with 23 three-line sayings (usually consisting of two lines in synonymous form, capped by a third line). There is even a ten-line unit: *i.e.* three 3-liners, clinched by a final line. Likewise the Egyptian Onchsheshonqy, nearly two millennia later, freely varies his lengths and styles, from several linked verses in synthetic parallelism down to the brevity of single-line aphorisms, shorter than anything in Proverbs. He also speaks as often in the imperative as in the indicative, and varies these forms with ejaculations ('Oh that . . .'). All this should warn us against undue reliance on the length and form of sayings as a means of dating them.

In content, too, the earthy and the elevated rub shoulders in early and late collections alike. The old Sumerian sayings can show considerable sympathy with the poor and a high regard for what Gordon calls 'cosmic and immutable values' such as truth and justice:

'Whoever has walked with truth generates life'[1]

– but are equally interested in the quirks of human character: the grumbler, the spendthrift, the priest with a parsonic voice, the palace and its wayward moods, and so on; just as Proverbs has an eye for the absurd as well as for the admirable.

If we expect the Egyptian Onchsheshonqy, at his late date, to have reached spiritual heights beyond his predecessors of the old Instruction manuals, we shall be disappointed, for the simple reason that he is not training public servants but coining sagacious sayings. Some of these will have a high moral tone: *e.g.* in praise of honesty,

'Do not speak with two voices:
speak truth to all men',

or of magnanimity,

'When your enemy entreats you,
do not conceal yourself from him'.

Some will be religious, whether with a view to reward,

'Serve your god, that he may protect you',

or purely to what is fitting,

'Do not pray to God and neglect what he says'.

[1] E. I. Gordon, *op. cit.*, p. 48.

But the great majority of his sayings are the shrewd reflections of a countryman with few illusions: as wary and salty as any folk-wisdom.

'All this', remarks Gemser, 'means a warning against constructing an evolutionary straight line of development of Egyptian wisdom and proverbial literature. Its less developed products do not necessarily stand at the beginning. They can accompany and be contemporary with the highest specimens of thought and feeling. . . . The lesson . . . has its significance also for the dating and the reconstruction of the history of Biblical proverb books and collections.'[1]

Yet once again, the urge to plot a progress of ideas and attitudes is not easily discouraged. To take a comparatively recent and diligently argued example, the commentary by McKane reviews the arguments and evidence to which Gemser, Kayatz and others appeal (as above), but replies that the history of thought in Egypt and elsewhere does not have to be paralleled in Israel. McKane therefore constructs his own evolutionary scheme for the sentence-sayings in Proverbs, rejecting the idea that different emphases in the material reflect either different coexisting circles of thought or different aspects of a single coherent view of wisdom.[2] Instead, he picks out of the uncoordinated mass of sayings those which he calls 'Class A', as products of the 'old wisdom' – that of the sages whom the prophets supposedly criticized for their impatience of revelation and their empirical approach to life. In contrast, he isolates 'Class C' sayings, which use 'God-language' or show other signs of Yahwistic piety (*e.g.* by classifying people as 'righteous' or 'wicked'), and sees these as a 'reinterpretation' of the 'older, empirical, mundane wisdom represented by the Class A material'.[3] This shift, he believes, took place shortly before the exile, when Israel's wise men 'were beginning to come to terms with Yahwism'.[4] The 'Class B' sayings come, by implication, between these two stages, and are marked by their interest in the *social* effects of good or bad behaviour.

In defence of this reconstruction, which imposes a maze-like pattern on his commentary, McKane points to the contrasting uses of particular words in different sayings. For example, words for schemes and plans are used now in a

---

[1]B. Gemser, 'The Instructions of Onchsheshonqy and Biblical Wisdom Literature', *VTS* 7 (1959), p.128 (102–128). The sayings quoted above are drawn from this article, which is also reprinted in *SAIW*, pp. 134–160.
[2]W. McKane, *Proverbs*, pp. 19–21.   [3]*Ibid.*, p.17.   [4]*Ibid.*, p.19.

good sense, now in a bad. Bribery is now approved, now condemned.[1] Man's intelligence is treated now with respect, now with reserve; or the teacher's instruction is likened to a fountain of life at one point, whereas elsewhere it is the fear of the LORD which is so described.

Not every reader will be convinced that these differing emphases in Proverbs represent strata deposited in different ages, rather than facets of truth enjoyed from different angles.

In passing it may be noted that McKane finds counter-parts to his A, B and C types of material also in chapters 1 – 9, and accordingly sees further evidence that his 'old wisdom' gave place to a more pious outlook, although he cannot accept Whybray's textual speculations in support of this.[2]

Is there a progression in the Solomonic sayings?

There have been various attempts to reduce these two collections (10:1 – 22:16, and 25 – 29) to some recognizable overall pattern or progression. One fairly noticeable division is between chapters 10 – 15 (where nearly all the sayings are antithetical, hinged on the 'but' of the second line – which R. B. Y. Scott takes to have been the pupils' set response to their teacher's opening) and chapters 16 to 22:16 where a saying's second line more often echoes or builds on the first. Another is between 25 – 27, in the collection made for Hezekiah, and 28 – 29 in the rest of that collection. In style, chapters 25 – 27 tend to group sayings together by subject-matter, and sometimes to expand a couplet into a quatrain. In content, 28 – 29 give some prominence to the social effects of moral attitudes.

But none of these features persists throughout a whole section, nor is there much agreement over the conclusions to be drawn from them about the relative ages or distinctive outlooks of these rough groupings. McKane in fact distrusts the term 'collection' if it is taken to mean a coherent group, since the essence of the sentence-saying is its self-contained individuality; and his distrust is not lessened by the dis-

---

[1]*Ibid.*, pp. 17f. This is the most plausible of McKane's 'differing attitudes'. But while bribery is morally condemned in Pr. 17:23, the remaining references are not normative but descriptive – both of its immediate attractions (17:8; 18:16; 21:14) and of its hidden damage (15:27). To say that this practice is anywhere 'recommended' is to mistake candour for persuasion.

[2]*Ibid.*, pp. 8, 240. On Whybray's study of Pr. 1 – 9, see above, pp.40f.

parity between his findings (based on the statistics of his three classes of sayings) and those of other scholars which are based on a broad view of large blocks of material. Whereas Skladny, for example, sees four collections of sayings whose respective tendencies point to the sequence 10 – 15; 28 – 29; 16 – 22:16; 25 – 27; McKane's statistics show a virtual absence of what he regards as 'late' material in the last of these groups, and a strong presence of such sayings in the first of them.[1] These quite opposite pictures suggest at first sight the advantage of a severely statistical analysis over a less rigorous approach; but the ultimate disagreement lies in the realm of opinion: that is, in opposite personal estimates of what is early material and what is late. Where McKane, as shown above, sees the frequent black-and-white contrasts in chapters 10 – 15 between the fortunes of the righteous and the wicked as reflections of a late religious dogmatism, Skladny finds in this 'naïvely optimistic' outlook a sign of an *early* stage of reflection on the way the world works.[2]

Support from other writers can be found for both these estimates of the relative ages of these groups of chapters, and for other variations as well – which implies that the search for theological progress or regress within these sayings is an inconclusive exercise. A more realistic approach is to treat the differences of tone and pitch not as chronological talking-points but as voices in counterpoint, each necessary to the other. The more-or-less random distribution of the sayings offers a resistance to schemes of grading, which it seems appropriate to respect.

One may add that non-evolutionary approaches to organizing this material on any large scale go equally against the grain of it – whether one thinks of Delitzsch's attempt to use the sayings on 'a wise son' as section-markers in chapters 10ff. (*i.e.* at 10:1; 13:1; 15:20)[3], or of P. Skehan's elaborate theory that the total of 375 sayings in 10:1 – 22:16 was determined by the numerical value of Solomon's name (achieved by the editor's insertion of enough extra proverbs

---

[1]In Pr. 25 – 27 (Skladny's latest group), McKane finds 'old wisdom' (his 'Class A' sayings) overwhelming the rest with over 80% of the material, while the latest stratum ('Class C') has less than 2½%. In 10 – 15 his figures are: Class A 47½%, B 17%, C 35½%. For the complete table, see McKane, p.12.

[2]U. Skladny, *Die ältesten Spruchsammlungen in Israel* (Göttingen, 1962), p.78.

[3]F. Delitzsch, *Proverbs* (Eng. edn, T. & T. Clark, 1884), I, p.326.

at the junction of chapters 15 and 16 to bring the two
component sections up to strength), and that the grand total
of lines in the whole book could be correlated with the value
of the three proper names in Proverbs 1:1.[1] Such ingenuity
seems overdone, especially since the two grand totals narrowly fail to coincide.

Solomon and the sentence-sayings

An appreciation of Solomon's drive to modernize his kingdom, of his leanings towards Egypt, and of the influence of
Egyptian Instruction manuals on the style of Proverbs 1 – 9,
has modified the former tendency to distrust his claim to the
authorship or editorship of any part of the book. Speaking of
the two Solomonic collections of sayings (10 – 22:16, and 25
– 29), W. Baumgartner observed that 'There is now again
more disposition to treat seriously the ascription of both to
Solomon . . .'.[2] Most scholars, however sceptical, will allow
that there must be at least some basis to the tradition.[3]

However, the tradition of a great burst of intellectual
activity in this king's reign – the 'Solomonic Enlightenment'
– is not unchallenged. R. B. Y. Scott questioned it in an
article in *VTS* 3 (1955) entitled 'Solomon and the Begin-
nings of Wisdom in Israel', arguing that the descriptions in
1 Kings of Solomon's superlative wealth and encyclopaedic
knowledge (as against his more modest gift of judicial
insight, described by the 'Deuteronomic historian' in 1 Ki. 3)
are 'postexilic in date and legendary in character'.[4] He plays
down the intellectual influence of Egypt in this reign, and

[1]P. Skehan, 'A Single Editor for the Whole Book of Proverbs' (*CBQ
Monographs* 1, 1971, pp.15–26; reprinted in Crenshaw, *SAIW*, pp.
329–340).

[2]W. Baumgartner, 'The Wisdom Literature', in H. H. Rowley (ed.), *The
Old Testament and Modern Study* (Oxford University Press, 1951), p.213.

[3]With fewer inhibitions, and the wealth of Near Eastern texts as a
control, K. A. Kitchen points out the inconsistency of a readiness to accept
as authentic the named authors of extra-biblical ancient texts on the one
hand, along with a certain hesitancy over biblical ascriptions on the other
hand, despite the cultural milieu largely common to both. See, *e.g.*, his
Ancient Orient and Old Testament, pp.136, 172.

[4]Scott (pp.268ff.) claims linguistic support for his adjective 'postexilic';
but W. M. W. Roth queries some of his examples and, in any case, his
assumption that they would prove the underlying *tradition* to be fictitious
(*VTS* 13 (1965), p.24). Scott's epithet, 'legendary', rests on his impression of
the 'extravagant' and 'grandiose' accounts of the king and his kingdom in
1 Ki. 4:29ff. (=5:9ff., Heb.) and 1 Ki. 10, which he cannot reconcile with
the strictures of ch. 11.

sees, instead, the reign of Hezekiah as the time when Judah felt the first real impact of it. It was Hezekiah, he suggests ('the *only* pre-exilic king after Solomon whose name has literary associations', p.277), who built up the picture of Solomon the Wise – an inference from Solomon's wealth, still visible in his buildings – to reinforce the image of his own era as a re-flowering of Solomon's golden age.

J. L. Crenshaw not only concurs with Scott in regarding Solomon's reputation as 'legendary', but appears to make the existence of *subsequent* legends (*e.g.* from Arabic and Christian sources) an argument for that verdict – for he devotes several pages of his *Old Testament Wisdom: an Introduction* to retailing them in all their fantastic detail. This can hardly be for mere entertainment; indeed he reveals how these tales affect his judgment, in the remark, 'An impregnable mountain called Fantasy stands between biblical interpreters and the historical Solomon' (p.44). At the risk of sounding glib it seems fair to say that this is a mountain on which a mustard-seed of faith would be well employed – that is, the modest degree of faith which is prepared to view the biblical account without extraneous distractions, and without undue prejudice against the phenomena of Solomon's wayward genius and flawed piety. The record in 1 Kings, instead of being discredited by its extremes of praise and blame, can be seen as a mirror to Solomon's enormous contradictions, doing justice to both the affluence and the tyranny he introduced to Israel, and to both the dazzling gifts he enjoyed and the tragically uneven use he made of them. If ever a king deserved the epigram, '. . . who never said a foolish thing, nor ever did a wise one', it was the Solomon whose spoilt brilliance is faithfully portrayed in 1 Kings, and frankly assessed in Ecclesiastes and in the enigmatic glimpses of his pomp in the Song of Solomon, but whose words – like many a preacher's – put his deeds to shame.

This still leaves as an open question the precise implications of the expression 'the proverbs of Solomon', and of the statement in 1 Kings 4:32 (=5:12, Heb.), 'he also uttered (lit. 'spoke') three thousand proverbs' – that is, to what extent these are sayings which he composed and sayings which he compiled, and what part he played in re-shaping aphorisms into the verse-couplets which are the norm in his two collections. What is certainly affirmed is that we have as Scripture only a fraction of one genre of his literary output.

Agur's confession and the numerical sayings of Proverbs 30

Agur's confession: Proverbs 30:1–9

The innocent reader of Proverbs 30 will find Agur refreshingly conscious (unlike his too-clever friends of verse 3) of his unfitness to speculate about God (2–4), to improve on God's word (5–6), or to steer a straight course unaided (7–9). In the rest of the chapter it is then no surprise to find him turning an equally honest and enquiring gaze upon the world about him, seeing it as sharply as he has seen himself.

There is now something of a critical consensus, however, that Agur's words should be taken as ending abruptly at verse 3 or verse 4, making him an agnostic or an outright atheist, to whom a new voice replies in verses 5–6, adding a suitable prayer in 7–9. The rest of the chapter is then attributed to yet another hand.

The grounds for this are precarious at every point.

a. Textually there is no basis for it. Even LXX, which places this chapter before chapter 25, and interrupts it with the 'further sayings of the wise' (24:23–34), creates this interruption after our verse 14, not at either of the suggested changes of voice.

b. The agnosticism of verses 2–4 is too reminiscent, in verse 4, of the lesson God dealt out to Job, and too ironical in verses 2–3 at the expense of the over-confident, to be taken as a gesture of despair rather than a lead-in to the constructive humility of verses 5ff. To deny one's power to search out God (2–4),[1] and to accept one's fallibility as both pupil (5–6) and worshipper (7–9) – these are thoroughly orthodox confessions. To drive a wedge between them is a gratuitous distortion.

c. The portrait of Agur as an atheist rests on a conjectural emendation of the obscure verse 1, to make it read (instead of 'to Ithiel, to Ithiel and Ucal') 'There is no God, there is no God, and I am exhausted'. This involves not only revocalizing the consonants, as do most other conjectures, but turning this verse (alone!) 'back' into Aramaic,[2] and viewing

---

[1]NEB obscures this by rendering 3b 'Nor have I *received* knowledge *from* the Holy One' (my italics) – as though Agur were as dubious of revelation as of reason. Literally it reads, 'nor know (or, 'so that I might know') knowledge of (the) holy one(s)'.

[2]*I.e., lā' 'iṭay 'ēl*, 'there is no God.' *Cf.* the Aramaic of Dn. 3:29c.

its present Hebrew form as a deliberate disguise of its
heretical sentiments.

So tortuous a hypothesis, to yield so startling a sense, is
understandably left aside by even the more adventurous of
modern translations, but is favoured for its ingenuity and
daring by some commentators.[1]

The numerical sayings in Proverbs 30:10–33

Two intensive studies of this form were published within
two years of one another, by G. Sauer and W. M. W. Roth in
1963 and 1965.[2] Both of these range far beyond Proverbs 30,
to study the roles of particular numbers and of numerical
series in the Old Testament and in neighbouring lit-
eratures, whether in narratives (*e.g.* the sevens in the
encircling of Jericho; or the sequences in the Keret legend
from Ugarit[3]), or in oracles and sayings such as 'For three
transgressions . . . and for four . . .' in Amos 1:3 – 2:8; or the
six . . . seven abominations in Proverbs 6:16–19, and the six
. . . seven troubles in Job 5:19ff.,[4] or again in lists of duties
such as the decalogues or dodecalogues of Exodus 20 or 34,
etc.

Of the two authors, Sauer is chiefly interested in de-
monstrating the literary affinity of Proverbs 30 with North
Canaanite and perhaps Edomite culture (*cf.* the Job-like
traits of verses 1–4), and with placing it at a stage between a
primitive unreadiness for numerical series and a later preoccupation with mathematical precision. Both these lines
point, for him, to the pre-exilic period, starting with Solomon and his cosmopolitan outlook and his interest in
nature-sayings.

Roth goes further than Sauer into questions of the deriv-
ation and function of this literary genre, noting opinions
that it was a teaching device (Hempel), or a development
from the riddle (Torczyner, 1924, followed by several other

---

[1]See R. B. Y. Scott, *in loc.*; W. McKane, *in loc.*; J. L. Crenshaw, *Old
Testament Wisdom*, p. 203.

[2]G. Sauer, *Die Sprüche Agurs* (*BWANT* 84, 1963); W. M. W. Roth,
Numerical Sayings in the Old Testament: a form-critical study (*VTS* 13,
1965).

[3]*E.g.* '. . . who had 7 brethren, 8 mother's sons' (KRT A i 8,9); *cf.* the
descending fractions $\frac{1}{3}$, $\frac{1}{4}$, $\frac{1}{5}$, $\frac{1}{6}$, $\frac{1}{7}$ in lines 16–20; *etc.* (Text in *ANET*,
pp.143ff.).

[4]*Cf.* the two . . . three banquets which Baal hates: *ANET*, p.132 (iii)
17–21.

writers, including Eissfeldt and Bentzen), or from the category of Nature-Wisdom seen in the name-lists (onomastica) of Mesopotamia and Egypt, and in Job 38 (Alt, 1951, followed by, *e.g.*, Weiser and von Rad). He also discusses what Dornsieff (1935) calls the *priamel*, *'i.e.*, a series of examples assembled to prove a point' – as in Amos 3:3–6, where seven cases lead up to the point finally made in the eighth.

Summing up his findings on these suggestions, Roth's view is that while the reflective numerical saying often has much in common with the 'priamel', it puts an emphasis, unlike the latter, on the actual number of the instances which it brings together. It also goes beyond the entertainment value of the riddle, and the purely mnemonic or encyclopaedic interest of a teaching device or onomasticon, to provide a means towards a 'mastery of life and the world' (p.96). It coordinates what it observes 'into a comprehensible list, defined with reference to its *content* through the common element of the items listed, and with reference to its *extent* through the numerical value' (p.95; my italics).

For some observations on the content of the sayings in Proverbs 30, see above, pp.34f.

The acrostic on wifely excellence
Proverbs 31:10–31

There are some general remarks on this passage on p.36, above. Here we need only comment briefly on its position in the book and on its acrostic form. As to its position, the LXX agrees with the Hebrew text in placing it last, but separates it from verses 1–9 by five chapters – which suggests that the words of Agur, the numerical sayings in chapter 30, the words of Lemuel (31:1–9) and the present passage may have circulated separately from one another before their inclusion in Proverbs. It also suggests that the poem is anonymous, rather than a continuation of the advice given to King Lemuel; and this is borne out by verse 23, where the woman's husband owes his honoured position not to heredity but to success.

As regards the alphabetic acrostic: the occurrence of this form is too widespread to throw any light on the date of the passage. There are four such poems in the first book of the psalter; another four (including the elaborate Ps.119) in the fifth book, and four in Lamentations 1 – 4. In Mesopotamian literature the outstanding example of an acrostic is the Babylonian Theodicy[1] with twenty-seven stanzas, each consisting of eleven identically initialled lines. The whole acrostic forms a sentence, not an alphabet, spelling out the author's name and credentials. By the side of this, most of the Hebrew examples are comparatively simple, their alphabetic form serving perhaps as an aid to memory and as a stimulus to the poet to cover his subject resourcefully and with a suggestion of comprehensiveness. This 'A to Z', so to speak, of wifely excellence makes a satisfying coda to the book.

[1]Text in *ANET*, pp.601–604. W. G. Lambert suggests a date *c.*1000, but 'no strong reason to compel any date in particular between about 1400 and 800' (*Babylonian Wisdom Literature* (Oxford University Press, 1960), pp. 63, 67).

4

The book of Job
A world well managed?

Even in our encounter with Proverbs it emerged that our best and soundest recipes for success can only be provisional, since our management of life is limited by what exists around us,[1] within us,[2] and, decisively, above us.[3] 'How then can man understand his way?' (Pr. 20:24) was a question which even that book of confident answers had to raise at some point.

But in Job, what was no more than a passing cloud in Proverbs now blots out the very sky. Instead of a simple reminder of human ignorance, what faces us here is the urgent problem of divine justice. The title of this chapter draws attention to that disturbing, indeed presumptuous, question about God. But in parallel with it, and hidden from the characters in the story, there is an equally unsettling question about man. In the human scene, is there any such thing as disinterested virtue? Does God's finest servant, his boasted showpiece, Job, serve him for conscience or convenience?

It is this that sets the story in motion.

An outline of the book

1. Prose Prologue (chs. 1 and 2): the cynic's taunt

The Satan suggests that the religion of so prosperous a

---

[1] *E.g.* the good or bad régimes glimpsed at intervals in, especially, Pr. 28 and 29.

[2] 'Even in laughter the heart may grieve' (Pr. 14:13, NEB; *cf.* 14:10).

[3] See the variations on the theme of 'Man proposes, God disposes': *e.g.* Pr. 16:1,9; 19:21; 21:30.

man as Job is sheer self-interest. He is given leave to test Job to the limit.

2. *Poetic Dialogue* (3:1 – 42:6): the sufferer's outrage, the moralists' bias, and the LORD's high wisdom.

   a. Job's lament (3).

   b. Three rounds of speeches by Job's comforters, punctuated by Job's protests (4 – 27) and followed by a poem on man's search for wisdom (28) and by Job's apologia (29 – 31).

   c. Elihu's interruption (32 – 37).

   d. The LORD enlarges Job's horizon (38 – 41).

   e. Job bows to his divine Lord's will (42:1–6).

3. *Prose Epilogue* (42:7-end): Job is vindicated and restored.

The literary aspect of this sequence of prose – poetry – prose, which has prompted many theories about the book's composition, is discussed in a later chapter, pp.77ff. What concerns us here is the fact that each part makes its contribution to the theological richness of the book, as well as to the progress of the plot. So it will be convenient to look at each of them in turn, in the order in which they appear.

Issues in the Prologue: Job 1 and 2

1. Suffering and sin

Once and for all, these opening scenes make it clear that suffering does not necessarily imply any guilt in the victim, nor any failure in his precautions or in his faith. Whatever rash things Job will later say and have to unsay, and whatever sins he may have already committed like the rest of us, the Prologue makes it plain that his suffering precedes the former and is unrelated to the latter. So far from guilt, it is his very innocence that has exposed him to the ordeal, as God's reiterated praise of him makes doubly clear (1:8; 2:3).

This already distinguishes the book of Job from its non-biblical neighbours;[1] but it does more. In the words of H. H. Rowley,

[1]See below, pp.132ff.

'By insisting that there is such a thing as innocent suffering the author of Job is bringing a message of the first importance to the sufferer. The hardest part of his suffering need not be the feeling that he is deserted by God, or the fear that all men may regard him as cast out from God's presence. If his suffering may be innocent it may not spell isolation from God, and when he most needs the sustaining presence of God he may still have it.'[1]

Indeed, to quote Rowley again,

'We may pause to note that the cause of Job's suffering was more than the Satan's insinuation against him. He was suffering to vindicate more than himself. He was vindicating God's trust in him. He was not so much abandoned by God as supremely honoured by God.'[2]

2. The Accuser

The scene in which the angels and the adversary alike present themselves to report on their activities expresses in vividly dramatic form the sole authority of God, whose ends even the rebellious unintentionally serve. The point is further emphasized in that the Hebrew treats the word Satan here not as a name but as a common noun, 'the satan', to indicate the place he is allowed to occupy in the total scheme of things. In a trial at law, the *śāṭān*, or 'adversary', is a term for an accuser or prosecutor,[3] and in the present context this creature's cynicism fits him to produce the most damning charge that can be brought. He will be no merely academic 'devil's advocate' but the real thing. If he can prove God's finest man a hypocrite, no-one's sincerity will still be credible. But if he fails in this test-case, with every weapon granted him, he will have shown, despite himself, that such a thing as pure disinterested godliness indeed exists, beyond all doubt and all concealing.

This brings us to the next point.

---

[1]H. H. Rowley, 'The Book of Job and its Meaning', in *From Moses to Qumran* (Lutterworth, 1963), p.178.

[2]*Ibid.*, pp.176f.

[3]*Cf.* Ps. 109:6b, RSV/NIV and mg.; also Zc. 3:1–2. In each of these references 'satan' has the definite article, as in Job. Satan appears as a proper name only once in the Old Testament (1 Ch.21:1).

3. Divine permission

It would be a mistake to see the concession to the accuser as a merely isolated tactic. It reflects the consistent practice of God. Where we might wish to argue that omnipotence ought to have stamped out evil at its first appearance, God's chosen way was not to crush it out of hand but to wrestle with it; and to do so in weakness rather than in strength, through men more often than through miracles, and through costly permissions rather than through flat refusals. Putting the matter in our own terms we might say that he is resolved to overcome it in fair combat, not by veto but by hard-won victory.

What the prologue makes clear, however, is that this is indeed permission, not abdication; for in both these chapters it is God who sets the limits of the test. The conditions are all that the challenger could desire (for nothing would be proved or disproved by Job's death, 2:6), but they are of God's choosing, not his. Likewise, at the end, it will be God who calls a halt to it – as it will be also (we may add) at the end of history.[1]

At the same time, we are not spared the jolt of the words, 'Behold, he is in your power' (2:6). And if the book of Job is meant to be a window on the world, rather than a door that shuts us in to an old debate, such words should be read against the background of the world we know: one which has seen in our own century enough divine permissions to make the blood run cold. By the side of the six million Jews of Hitler's holocaust, to say nothing of the still more numerous victims of other tyrants of our time, or those of natural disasters, the bereavements and sufferings of Job may look almost negligible, and his bewilderment more than matched by ours, although ours will take a different form from his. With hindsight we may easily see through the fallacies of his friends' theology, but we are as incapable as Job himself of fathoming the mystery of what God allows, and why.

What we have, however, is a New Testament echo of the prologue, which confirms the doctrine of divine permission, but does so in the illuminating context of the Passion. The words are Christ's:

'Simon, Simon, take heed: Satan has been given leave to sift all of you like wheat; but for you I have prayed that

---

[1] Jas. 5:7–11 draws this analogy from the case of Job.

your faith may not fail; and when you have come to yourself, you must lend strength to your brothers.'[1]

Significantly, the Son's counter-plea to that of Satan was not
that the test should be forbidden: only that it should be
fruitful. But further, the context of his servants' ordeal, the
fact that their Master himself would not be spared, supplies
an element which is necessarily missing from our prologue.
The God who handed over Job to his torturer was no
olympian figure, content to win his victories through others.
He would say, in Christ, to his own more hideous tor-
mentors,

'This is your hour, and the power of darkness.'[2]

Any thinking about divine sufferance of evil, and exposure
of the innocent to grief, must take its bearings now from
that crucial and seminal event.

Voices in the Dialogue: Job 3:1 – 42:6

A rather obvious but convenient approach will be to listen to
each in turn of the three main contributions to the counter-
point of this great section: that is, to the themes of Job's
companions (including Elihu), of Job himself, and of the
LORD.

1. Job's comforters

It is possible to dismiss these friends of Job too lightly, for
the book does not present them as hypocrites arriving to
gloat (see 2:11–13), nor as heretics offering manifestly false
doctrines, nor again as fools producing no serious arguments. The New Testament can treat certain words of Eliphaz as Scripture;[3] and every speaker believes firmly in the
one God, who is not only all-powerful but wholly just, and at
the same time quick to restore the penitent and to heap
blessings on the teachable.

> For he wounds, but he binds up;
> he smites, but his hands heal.
>
> 5:18 (*cf.* 17–27).

Their outlook chimes in very largely with the promises and

---

[1]Lk. 22:31–32, NEB.   [2]Lk. 22:53.
[3]*Cf.* Jb. 5:13 with 1 Cor. 3:19; and *cf.* Jb. 5:17 with Heb. 12:5.

warnings of the law, especially Deuteronomy, and with the wisdom of Proverbs and the moral standpoint of the Prophets. Yet these men are 'miserable comforters', not only in Job's estimation (16:2) but even more strongly in God's (42:7–9). In view of this, one may easily conclude that the book of Job is designed as an attack on the older wisdom school, embodied in these men, and indeed on the whole concept of divine rewards and punishments.

This, however, is too sweeping. A closer look at the material shows that the basic error of Job's friends is that they overestimate their grasp of truth, misapply the truth they know, and close their minds to any facts that contradict what they assume. That being so, if the book is attacking anything its target is not the familiar doctrines of other Scriptures, such as God's justice and benevolence, his care for the righteous and punishment of the wicked, or the general law that what one sows one reaps. Rather, it attacks the arrogance of pontificating about the *application* of these truths, and of thereby misrepresenting God and misjudging one's fellow men. To put it more positively, the book shows (by its context, the opening scene in heaven) how small a part of any situation is the fragment that we see; how much of what we do see we ignore or distort through preconceptions; and how unwise it is to extrapolate from our elementary grasp of truth.

Job's well-meaning comforters demonstrate the force of this by straying ever further from reality as they pursue their fixed ideas of suffering as punitive or, at best, purgative. Shocked, instead of shaken, by Job's denials that his suffering is deserved, they pass from gentle probings for some hidden sin, to stern rebukes for his intemperate language (*e.g.* ch. 15), and finally to inventing a fictitious catalogue of crimes for him (22:5ff.). To reinforce this, they paint idealized pictures of a world of prosperous saints and destitute sinners, brushing aside all contrary examples.[1] And to magnify God's holiness they are driven to adding to it the element of royal disdain, so that he distrusts the very angels, finds fault with the starry skies, and regards humanity as worms and maggots (15:15f.; 25:5f.). Small wonder that in the epilogue God charges them with folly and slander (42:8).

One of the lessons of the book, therefore, is that God

---

[1] *E.g.* Job's poignant instances of wicked men triumphant (ch.21) and the innocent exploited (ch.24).

abhors our special pleading for him, with its suppression of unwelcome facts. The point is powerfully put by Job:

> Will you speak falsely for God,
>   and speak deceitfully for him?
> Will you show partiality toward him,
>   will you plead the case for God?
> Will it be well with you when he searches you out?
> Or can you deceive him, as one deceives a man?
>
> 13:7–9.

This is enough to give pause to any devious defender of orthodoxy – though before the unorthodox rejoice too much, they may reflect for their part that the arch-sceptic lost his case, and even Job his honest doubts.

On the specific issue of suffering, the basic mistake of these comforters is still with us wherever Christians make projections from their axioms about God, or from their doctrine of redemption, to the effect that the perfect health of the redeemed, here and now, must be what God intends. Like Job's comforters, those who argue in this way are deciding for themselves what God must surely think and do. Further, but unlike their predecessors, they are gripped by the '*now*' of God's promises, to the exclusion of his '*not yet*'.[1] Had they ministered to Job, they would have seen his plight not necessarily as a punishment or (with Elihu) an education,[2] but rather as a consequence of drifting somewhat from the LORD and from the full enjoyment of his saving health. It would be a situation to be remedied by faith. Yet Job's sufferings were in fact brought on him not by any lapse of faith but by his very blamelessness; and their long duration was serving heaven's own secret purposes, including the completion of the test and the exhausting of the human arguments. This is not to say that his case should be seen as the key to all others, or even to any others: simply that it lifts one corner of a curtain beyond which, at any time, there will lie factors of which we have no inkling.

---

[1]*E.g.*, appeal is made to Is. 53:4 to show that our sicknesses as well as our sins were cancelled at the cross, and therefore must be borne by us no longer. But that prophecy, 'he took our infirmities and bore our diseases', is cited in Mt. 8:17 as fulfilled in the Galilean healing ministry. That these healings were but a foretaste of the physical side of our redemption, for which '*we wait . . ., we wait . . .*', is made especially clear by Rom. 8:18–25 (esp. 23–25), but also by the many passages which contrast our present bondage to decay with our future glory.

[2]*E.g.* Jb. 33:29f.; 34:32; 36:9f., 22.

But this brings us to Job himself, as he, above all, wrestles with his problem in the dark.

2. Job himself

In his perplexity, Job feels himself to be under attack from two quarters at once: from his friends and from his God. We may look at these two preoccupations in turn.

a. Job and his friends: the sting of misjudgment
From the first, he finds them exasperating, for he is wrestling with a question which to their minds he has no right to ask. To them, the issue he should be facing is 'What have I done?' – but to him it is 'What has *God* done? What has come over him?'

So his friends, like a cloud of flies, are an irritation, and his exchanges with them are indignant. He is *hurt* by their fault-finding: their failure to allow for his agony as they react to his desperate words:

> Do you think that you can reprove words,
>   when the speech of a despairing man is wind?
>
> 6:26.

He comes back at them with *sarcasm*:

> No doubt you are the people,
>   and wisdom will die with you.
>
> 12:2.

> What a fine help you are . . .
> You give such good advice
>   and share your knowledge with a fool like me!
>
> 26:2–3, GNB.

As we have seen already, he can be *accusing*:

> You cover up your ignorance with lies . . .
>   Do you think your lies will benefit God?
> Are you trying to defend him?
>
> 13:4a, 7b–8a, GNB.

Or *reproachful*, whether hotly or with pathos:

> If you and I were to change places,
> I could talk like you;
> how I could harangue you
> and wag my head at you!
> But no, I would speak words of encouragement,

> and then my condolences would flow in streams.
>> 16:4–5, NEB.

> Pity me, pity me, you that are my friends . . .
> Have you not had your teeth in me long enough?
>> 19:21–22, NEB.

Or again, bitterly *defiant*:

> . . . and after I have spoken, mock on.
>> 21:3.

But finally, utterly *contemptuous*:

> And you! You try to comfort me with nonsense!
> Every answer you give is a lie!
>> 21:34, GNB.

b. Job and his God: (i) his sense of outrage
It is Job's remembered intimacy with God, whose 'friendship
. . . was upon my tent' (29:4), but who has *'turned* cruel to
me' (30:21) – it is this that really hurts him. He had known
dark times before, but then he had had God's light to walk
by (29:3). So now there can be no question for him of merely
suffering in silence, like an animal or like a stoic. He must
find out what has happened between himself and God, for it
has all the marks of an estrangement – and silence is no
remedy for that. Indeed God's attitude appears to go beyond
coolness to a positive hostility, expressed in a ceaseless rain
of blows. Chapter 7 in particular, which captures the toss-
ings and turnings, the nightmares, the longing for death, of
a desperately sick man, has the added bitterness of a conviction that every throb and every terror comes immediately
from God.

> When I say, 'My bed will comfort me,
>   my couch will ease my complaint,'
> then thou dost scare me with dreams
>   and terrify me with visions.
>> 7:13–14.

It all seems so petty, so out of all proportion! Does God feel
threatened by him?

> Am I the sea, or a sea monster,
>   that thou settest a guard over me?
>> 7:12.

And has he no generosity? Must he come down on every little fault?

> If I sin, what do I do to thee, thou watcher of men? . . .
> Why dost thou not pardon my transgression
> and take away my iniquity?
>> 7:20a,21a (*cf.* 10:14–15; 13:23–26).

For this is bullying, not punishment!

> Why hast thou made me thy butt,
> and why have I become thy target?
>> 7:20b, NEB (*cf.* 16:9–17).

Is it even possible (as Job seems to ask in his next speech) that God created and preserved him for this very purpose? That his seeming kindness was 'calculated cruelty'?[1]

> Thou hast granted me life and steadfast love;
> and thy care has preserved my spirit.
> Yet these things thou didst hide in thy heart;
> I know that this was thy purpose.
>> 10:12–13.

These desperate perplexities are summed up in a bitter parody of the question of Psalm 8:4, no longer asked in adoration:

> What is man that thou makest much of him
> and turnest thy thoughts towards him,
> only to punish him morning by morning
> or to test him every hour of the day?
>> 7:17–18, NEB.

The cataract of protest grows in volume and intensity to the end of Job's apologia in chapter 31. But he is not reacting as the Accuser had hoped. Nowhere does he turn round and say, in effect, 'Then I have finished with goodness and with God!' Instead, even his initial longing to be left in peace gives way to a growing ambition to fight his way through to God and argue the whole thing out with him. From chapter 9 and onwards many of his most poignant sayings are wrung from him by his alternate longing for and shrinking from this imagined confrontation.

> Oh, that I knew where I might find him,
> that I might come even to his seat!

---

[1]Rowley, on 10:13. For a contrary view, that the mention of 'steadfast love' expresses Job's 'struggling faith', see Andersen, p.154.

> I would lay my case before him
> and fill my mouth with arguments.
>
> 23:3–4.

For at one moment he is all eagerness:

> . . . he knows the way that I take;
> when he has tried me, I shall come forth as gold.
>
> 23:10.

> I would give him an account of all my steps;
> like a prince I would approach him.
>
> 31:37.

But at another he reflects that God is not a quarry he can catch, or a defendant he can bring to court – still less out-argue!

> Behold, I go forward, but he is not there;
> and backward, but I cannot perceive him . . .
>
> 23:8.

> If one wished to contend with him,
> one could not answer him once in a thousand times.
>
> 9:3.

And what if one *could* win the argument? What difference would it make?

> There is no umpire between us,
> who might lay his hand upon us both.
>
> 9:33.

> What he desires, that he does.
> For he will complete what he appoints for me;
> and many such things are in his mind.
> Therefore I am terrified at his presence . . .
>
> 23:13b–15a.

In this oscillation between hope and despair, but in the stubbornness with which he returns to the attack, no doubt remains about the thing that matters to Job above life itself: his integrity and its recognition by his Lord. Pressed by his friends to appease God by a trumped-up confession, he refuses with fine scorn:

> Far be it from me to say that you are right;
> till I die I will not put away my integrity from me.
>
> 27:5.

> Behold, he will slay me; I have no hope;[1]
> yet I will defend my ways to his face.
>
> 13:15.

So the satan's prediction has utterly failed. The deeper Job's darkness, the more his grip tightens on what he has always stood for, and the more doggedly he gropes for the way home. There had to be this obscurity for the test to be true. Yet, in the nature of things, Job's could not be the total darkness of the pagan or the atheist, for the memory of God's truth and goodness was still there, to break surface at some of the most unlikely moments.

c. Job and his God: (ii) his glimmers of hope

We have already noticed (in Job's rebuke to his friends for their specious arguments, 13:7–12) his conviction that God would have no truck with anything untrue – a conviction which unconsciously contradicted his own suspicion, in a dark moment, that 'though I am blameless, he would prove me perverse' (9:20b). *In his bones, Job knew what God stood for.* And this surely must include (as he hoped against hope) some shred of compassion! Why, Job's own care for the destitute had been spurred by the account which he knew he must tender to God – for as a heartless man 'I could not have faced his majesty' (31:13–23). Even the fearful surmise that God had made him on purpose to torment him (if such is the thrust of the enigmatic 10:13)[2] was voiced within a prayer that was at least half convinced that his Creator's former 'steadfast love' and 'care' (10:12) were genuine, and that his compassion could even now be touched:

> Remember that thou hast made me of clay;
> and wilt thou turn me to dust again?
>
> 10:9.

For all its ebbing and flowing, that conviction inches its way forward, to reach a point, momentarily, in his next long utterance, where he finds himself unable to believe that God's strange wrath can last for ever. Most movingly he pleads:

---

[1]The first line of the verse may be speaking either in hope (AV, RV, NIV) or in desperation (RSV, NEB, GNB), since the first word (*hēn*) can mean either 'Behold' or 'Even if'. And while the written text has 'I do *not* (*lō'*) hope', a traditional reading of it is '*In him* (*lô*) I hope'. (*lō'* and *lô* sound alike.) Either way, the second line refuses to give ground.

[2]See above, p.65.

Oh that thou wouldest hide me in Sheol, . . .
    until thy wrath be past,
    that thou wouldest appoint me a set time,
        and remember me!
If a man die, shall he live again?
    All the days of my service I would wait,
    till my release should come.
Thou wouldest call, and I would answer thee;
    thou wouldest long for the work of thy hands.

14:13–15.

That high-water mark was soon to be surpassed in 16:18 –
17:3, where in a sudden surge of faith Job cries out,

Even now, behold, my witness is in heaven,
    and he that vouches for me is on high–

and where, in a magnificent paradox, he appeals to God
himself to plead his case with God!

My friends scorn me;
    my eye pours out tears to God,
that he would maintain the right of a man with God,
    like that of a man with his neighbour.

16:19–21.

This he clinches with a further appeal of equal paradox and
daring: that God, his creditor and judge, will be – of all
things! – his guarantor:

Lay down a pledge for me with thyself;
    who is there that will give surety to me?

17:3.

In the light of this, and of his vision of a day, however
distant, when God and he would be at one again (14:15),
there can be little doubt that when he speaks of his 'witness
. . . in heaven' (16:19) it is to God himself, not some unidenti-
fied third party, that he is looking. As he has just said, who
else is there to take his part?

That is the background to the greatest saying of all:

For I know that my Redeemer[1] lives,
    and at last he will stand upon the earth;[2]
and after my skin has been thus destroyed,

---

[1]Heb. *gō'ēl*, *i.e.* the person charged with the duty of avenging or
rehabilitating his kinsman.

[2]Lit. 'upon dust'; but 41:33 (25, Heb.) confirms the sense, 'upon earth'.

> then from[1] my flesh I shall see God,
> whom I shall see on my side,[2]
> and my eyes shall behold, and not another.
> My heart faints within me!
>
> 19:25–27.

Whatever else is of uncertain translation in this passage, two things at least are clear: that Job at this moment is sure of vindication, and equally sure that it will bring him face to face with God. He looks forward to it with conviction ('I know . . .') and with breathless awe ('My heart faints . . .'); but it is seemingly a distant prospect, beyond – perhaps far beyond – his death, as we gather from his concern that his words may not die with him but be indelible.[3] This agrees with his thought of having to be recalled, if need be, from Sheol for his reinstatement (14:13–17). It begins to appear that however fitfully and dimly he perceives it, he is speaking here of nothing less than resurrection. His cry, 'from my flesh I shall see God', has been traditionally taken to affirm this; and whatever ambiguity the expression, 'from my flesh', might have in isolation, it is clarified both by the construction in which it stands[4] and by the sequel to which it leads. In that sequel (verse 27) there is a triple emphasis on the fact that he will enjoy this moment of truth at first hand (not merely that posterity will see his name cleared), and that he will see God not in some metaphorical sense or incorporeal state, but with his very eyes.

Then the vision fades, and Job is left with the brute facts of his unmerited sufferings, his friends' reproaches and the world's intolerable wrongs, to reinforce his will to challenge God to justify what he is doing. On that defiant note, sustained in his remaining speeches to the end of chapter 31, he will at long last rest his case.

An interlude: the young Elihu

Whatever may be the literary history of the inclusion of Elihu's speeches between Job's challenge to the LORD and its

[1]In itself, *min*, 'from', can have various senses, including 'away from' – hence the rendering 'without my flesh' in the margins of RV, RSV; *cf.* NIV mg. But this overlooks the fact that elsewhere in the OT, *with verbs of seeing*, *min* always has the sense of 'from', never of 'without' or 'apart from' (*e.g.* Gn. 13:14; Jb. 36:25; Ps. 14:2; *etc.*)

[2]Or 'for myself'.   [3]See 19:23–24, leading into the 'Redeemer' saying.
[4]See again footnote 1, above.

answer,[1] the interruption has its own minor part to play in the pattern of the book. First, it delays the dénouement. We are kept waiting for the great moment of the LORD's reply, tantalized by a torrent of talk which promises enlightenment but offers in the event little more than eloquence. Secondly, in the end it is totally ignored. It does not even qualify for condemnation, as do the words of the three friends in 42:7–9. The effect of this, in the book as we are given it, is to imply that God has already heard more than enough of our well-meaning arguments, even before Elihu offers his opinions, and that any further contributions are simply not invited, from us or from anyone else.

To our ears, Elihu may sometimes seem to have a point, where he enlarges on the educative, cleansing effects that suffering may have (*e.g.* 33:14–30; 36:15). But Job's friend Eliphaz has said it long before, and in any case we know from the prologue that Job was suffering for quite another set of reasons, on which it was idle to speculate. If we needed any further warning against jumping to conclusions about particular cases, Elihu has certainly provided it.

3. The LORD's reply

So the LORD answers no-one but Job. That he speaks at all is itself an answer to one of Job's misgivings: that he will prove endlessly elusive, totally unapproachable.

But he answers out of the whirlwind – formidably, boisterously, never for a moment on the defensive. Job had pictured himself (given the chance) hurling arguments and challenges at him; but the boot is on the other foot. The entire reply is a stream of unanswerable questions, starting with the farthest reaches of time and space, and drawing ever narrowing circles round him of things beyond his knowing, even things as close at hand as the beasts and birds that he would have taken for granted.

Two things at least are happening here. First – and of immense significance – God has changed the subject. All the obsessive talk about Job's plight as punitive is left completely on one side. The inference could hardly be plainer: that Job and his friends have not only found the wrong answers; they have been asking the wrong questions. Indeed, what one writer has called the 'kindly playfulness'[2]

[1]See below, pp.81ff.

[2]Andersen, p. 271. *Cf.*, more sharply, J. W. Whedbee, 'The Comedy of Job', in *Semeia* 7 (1977), p.24.

of God's raillery ('surely you know!' – 'you were born then!')
puts Job in his place more as a father might do it to a
dogmatic adolescent than as a judge to an offender. Even
his direct rebukes, brusque as they are, are not concerned
with sins of the past: only with the ravings and tirades of
the present. Job's eventual penitence, we can note, is concerned with precisely this, at both 40:3–5 and 42:1–6.

> I lay my hand upon my mouth . . .
>
> 40:4.

> . . . I have uttered what I did not understand . . .
>
> 42:3.

Secondly, God is enlarging Job's horizon. The superb
poetry, which brings before him the majesty, beauty and
exuberance of the creation, invites him to explore in his
mind the great context of his being. It will – or should –
reassure him that his Maker is unimaginably wise and of
infinite resource; but it will also bring it home to him that
his ash-heap is not the centre or circumference of the
world, and that his perplexing role is intertwined with that
of innumerable others.

For, thirdly, there is nothing soothing or explanatory in
these chapters. The argumentative Job must do some better thinking, the princely challenger must listen to a
counter-challenge. If the first part of God's discourse has
made Job face his inevitable ignorance, the second part
(40:6 – 41:34) confronts him with his appointed littleness.
Can he play God, and put the world to rights? Does it look
for even a moment as if that were his place – and if not,
who is he to teach God his business?

> Cast one look at the proud and bring them low,
>   strike down the wicked where they stand. . . .
> I myself will be the first to acknowledge
>   that your own right hand can assure your triumph.
>
> 40:12, 14, JB.

Can he even take liberties with some of his fellow
creatures?

> Behold, Behemoth,
>   which I made as I made you.
>
> 40:15.

And what of Leviathan?

> Will you play with him as with a bird,
> or will you put him on leash for your maidens?

41:5.

> He beholds everything that is high;
> he is king over all the sons of pride.

41:34.

On that note of unflattering comparison the LORD's reply to Job concludes – perhaps to our surprise.[1] That a discourse which began with the cosmos should end in praise of two aquatic monsters, however fearsome, may strike us as eccentric; and that it should ignore our burning questions altogether may be a bitter disappointment.

But there is no mistaking the thrust of it, congenial or not. It cuts us down to size, treating us not as philosophers but as children – limited in mind, puny in body – whose first and fundamental grasp of truth must be to know the difference between our place and God's, and to accept it. We may reflect that if, instead of this, we were offered a defence of our Creator's ways for our approval, it would imply that he was accountable to us, not we to him. And if, not being offered this, we were to demand it, we should be guilty of the arrogance of Adam.

Job has no such pretensions any longer. Seeing God with newly opened eyes he has no questions, only a confession and a self-abasement that is as deep as his indignation had been high.

The Adam in us might have wished for a final speech by Job in terms somewhat as follows:

> '. . . but now I see it all;
> therefore, though pleased that I spoke out,
> I now withdraw the charge.'

Every line of it would have breathed the spirit of unregenerate man. Instead, this man whom nobody could muzzle is as forthright in his surrender as he had ever been in argument. Every line of it is unreserved:

> '. . . but now my eye sees thee;
> therefore I despise myself,
> and repent in dust and ashes.'

42:6.

[1]For some opinions on the status of chapters 40 – 41, see below, pp.83ff.

The Epilogue: Job 42:7–end

After nearly forty chapters of tempestuous poetry, the return to the simplicity of prose and to the idyllic setting in which the book had opened rounds off this masterpiece, one may feel, to perfection. On the other hand, some would see this as a descent from the sublime to at least the common-place, and more seriously, as a surrender to the simplistic outlook of Job's comforters on matters of reward and punishment. In purely aesthetic terms one could argue the case either way; but what of its theology?

Under the placid surface there is more than a mere relaxing of tension. First, there is the startling verdict of heaven against the efforts of Eliphaz and his friends to justify God's ways, and in favour of the gritty honesty of Job. We are forcibly reminded that God, for all his rough handling of his servant's rude demands, reads between the lines and listens to the heart. This has implications, too, for the way in which some other strained and bitter voices, in the Psalms and elsewhere, may need hearing.

Secondly, by appointing Job as intercessor for his misguided friends, and doing so while he was still unsightly and unhealed, God put it beyond all doubt that this man's sufferings were no disgrace, no punishment. What the prologue had made clear by the scene in heaven, that there is such a thing as undeserved affliction, the epilogue abundantly confirmed – yet without disclosing heaven's secret to the actors in the drama.

Thirdly, this same sequence – vindication before restoration – faithfully reflects Job's own order of priorities, revealed already in his stout refusal to buy off the supposed enmity of God and the torments of his sickness by a false confession. What mattered to him above anything that he had lost was God's recognition of his innocence; and God now shows that he takes him at his word. With this, Job's cup is full. The healing and prosperity that followed were no more than its overflowing.

Fourthly, it is a pregnant statement that the LORD restored Job's fortunes 'when he had prayed for his friends' (who by now had almost the status of enemies). For while nothing is directly made of this as an exercise of magnanimity, the fact remains that, had Job's vindication been the only end in view, it could have been achieved simply by the judgment God pronounced in verse 7; 'You (Eliphaz and your two friends) have not spoken of me what is right, as my servant Job has.' Instead, there is this further step, which not only emphasized the point already made, but led Job out of the imprisonment of self-preoccupation, and out of the deadlock of invective. Here was no arbitrary demand.

So the ending is unclouded. We may notice, if we will, the irony of the appearance on the scene, at long last, of Job's relations, with their belated condolences and their uniform tokens of regard. But there is no bitterness in the telling of it, and nothing but pleasure in the description of Job's many consolations in the rest of his long life.

Some, as we have noticed, would grudge him this serenity, preferring the starkness of pure tragedy to the easing of tension which they would regard as anticlimax. Job – and arguably even the book of Job as literature – would have fared ill at their hands! Certainly the epistle of James has no such reservations. 'You have all heard how Job stood firm, and you have seen how the Lord treated him in the end. For the Lord is full of pity and compassion.'[1]

That is the last word on the matter, both in the book of Job and in the New Testament's reflection on it. And that will be the last word in the bigger drama: not that man will demand and get his answers or his imagined rights, but that God will give, to those who endure to the end in this bitter war, 'such good things as pass man's understanding'.

[1]Jas. 5:11, NEB.

5

Job in academic discussion

This chapter will look at four areas of debate: first, the date of the book; secondly, the relation of the prose prologue and epilogue to the 'poetic dialogue'; thirdly, some problem passages in that dialogue; fourthly, the overall purpose and point of the book.

The date of the book

Since there are no historical reference-points for the book's composition, the suggested dates for it have ranged at will over nearly two millennia, from patriarchal to Hasmonean times.[1] The Talmud was even bold enough to name an author: Moses (Baba Bathra 14b). In recent scholarship, conjectures mostly keep to within a few centuries of the Exile, before or after. Among those who favour a post-exilic date are Dhorme (placing it between 500 and 450 BC), Rowley (nearer 400 than 500), Gordis (between 500 and 300), and Irwin (approximately the 4th century) – to name a few.[2] Grounds for a date in this period are partly linguistic, since Aramaic had become the lingua franca of the Persian empire, and Job has many Aramaisms; but partly also the case is argued from the contents of the book. Among the scholars just named, Dhorme holds that Zechariah influen-

---

[1] That is, from c. 2000 BC down to the 2nd or 1st century BC. But the existence of a Greek translation of Job, from the 1st century BC or earlier, and a very early Job Targum found in Cave XI at Qumran, make a date after c.300 BC most unlikely. See Gordis, *The Book of God and Man*, p.217; Andersen, p.55, for further details.

[2] For a list of over fifty scholars and opinions of all kinds, see Rowley, *From Moses to Qumran*, pp.173f., n.2.

ced the book, but Malachi was indebted to it;[1] Rowley finds
it probable that the perverse doctrine of Job's friends rested
mistakenly on themes from Deuteronomy, Jeremiah and
Ezekiel;[2] Gordis reckons that the author knew 'Deutero-
Isaiah', and that the figure of the Satan was perhaps derived
from Zoroastrianism;[3] while Irwin speaks more generally of
a maturity of outlook suggestive of a later rather than an
earlier Judaism.[4]

In favour of an earlier date, the argument against it from
Aramaisms (which could point either to a time or to a *place*
of origin) must now take into account on the other side a
number of apparently primitive forms (in the light of
Ugaritic) and old spellings.[5] J. C. L. Gibson, while suggesting a date only shortly before the Exile, remarks: 'Perhaps Job will be the next biblical book to be given back to
old Israel, as scholarship perceives that like the Psalms it
belongs to the time when the Hebrew-Canaanite poetic tradition was still a living one'.[6] M. H. Pope finds himself
'inclined to share Kaufmann's view that the book "was composed in the golden age of Israel's creativity, the age before
the Exile" '.[7] Scholars on both sides of the debate admit the
inconclusiveness of arguments from the history of ideas; and
Pope, while suggesting the 7th century as 'the best guess for
the date of the Dialogue', reminds us that if the eastern
Semites could discuss the problem of suffering as exten-
sively as they did in the second millennium BC, it 'gives
reason to suppose that the western Semites could have produced similar works at the same time'.[8] Comparably open-
minded, Andersen, who is inclined to see the book taking
shape substantially in the reign of Solomon, and 'its normative form settled by the time of Josiah', admits that it 'could
have been written at any time between Moses and Ezra'.[9]

Happily, this open question is academic, in every sense of
the word. This book is no prisoner of time.

[1]E. Dhorme, *Job*, p.clxix.
[2]*From Moses to Qumran*, p.174; *The Book of Job*, p.22.
[3]Gordis, *The Book of God and Man*, p. 216.
[4]*Peake's Commentary, Revised*, section 339 d.
[5]See Andersen, pp. 57 (with footnotes 1 and 3) and 62 (lines 3–5).
[6]*SJT* 28³ (1975), p. 260, n.2.
[7]Pope, p.xxxvi.
[8]*Ibid.*, p.xxxvii. He is referring to such works as the Sumerian 'Man
and his God'; The Babylonian Theodicy; Ludlul Bēl Nēmeqi. See below,
pp.132ff.
[9]Andersen, p.13.

The prose framework and poetic dialogue

The form of the book, as prose – verse – prose, is by no means unique (see, for instance, the Egyptian 'Dispute over Suicide', translated in *ANET*, pp. 405–407), but it has prompted much discussion and a general opinion that the poem has been set within the frame of an ancient story – either as retold by the author of the poem, or preserved in the form in which he found it. In favour of the latter view one can point to the contrast between the narrative's classical simplicity and the poem's rich vocabulary and frequent Aramaisms;[1] and in particular, to the fact that the speakers in the poetic dialogue use almost exclusively the terms Shaddai, El and Eloah for God, while the narrative speaks only of Elohim or Yahweh.[2] What some would also maintain is that the epilogue upholds the view of reward and punishment which the poem has refuted,[3] and that the narrative and the poem present two incompatible portraits of Job. This estimate of the man, however, is artificially static – as though his prolonged agony of mind and spirit had given him no questions to wrestle with after his initial acquiescence. As for Irwin's complaint that in the epilogue the Promethean Job of the poem submits too tamely for credibility or for admiration,[4] this fails to give due weight to the stupendous experience of '. . . now mine eye sees thee', or to the homesickness of Job for 'the friendship of God . . . when the Almighty was yet with me'.[5] It is a very different relationship from that of Prometheus to Zeus.

In 1896 Budde coined the term 'Das Volksbuch' for the postulated written story behind the book as we have it; and

---

[1]But note the apparent Aramaic loan-word for 'receive' (*qbl*, Pi.) in the prologue itself at 2:10. Note also N. H. Snaith's disagreement over the frequency of Aramaisms (Snaith, p.83, cited by Andersen, p.61, n.1).

[2]On the purely stylistic contrast, Dhorme remarks that 'one and the same man can tell a story when necessary and sing when necessary' (p.xv). On vocabulary, he adduces many points in common between the sections, and argues that the distribution of the divine names between the narrator on the one hand and the non-Israelite Job and company on the other hand reveals the purposeful skill of a single writer (p.lxxii). On the occasion in the prologue (1:21), and again in the poem (12:9) where Job himself speaks of 'Yahweh', Rowley has pointed out that Job, unlike his friends, is acknowledged by Yahweh as 'my servant' (1:8, *etc.*) (*From Moses to Qumran*, pp.155f.; *The Book of Job*, p.11).

[3]Against this charge, see above, pp.73f., and Rowley, *From Moses to Qumran*, pp.159f.; *The Book of Job*, pp.266f.

[4]*Peake's Commentary*, section 355 d.   [5]Jb. 42:5; 29:4–5.

the existence of a name for it probably encouraged certain writers to attempt a reconstruction of it. Cheyne published in 1898 an imaginary centrepiece to the prologue and epilogue, in synthetic Elizabethan English, in which it is the comforters who question heaven's justice and are rebuked by Job – a theory espoused in due course by several scholars, including Kraeling, Alt and Lindblom. On this, Rowley justly comments: 'This is mere modern fiction . . .'[1] Without going to these lengths, some writers have regarded the three friends of Job as the poet's invention for the purpose of the dialogue, having played no part in the prose narrative as it supposedly first stood. Gordis therefore credits the poet with composing the passages in the prologue and epilogue which refer to them,[2] and Fohrer outlines a six-stage operation by which the three comforters have taken the place of the kinsfolk and acquaintances of Job whom we now meet only in 42:11, and who were the original recipients of God's rebuke recorded in 42:7–10.[3]

These (to adapt a famous verse in Job) are but the outskirts of the writings on this matter, and how small a whisper of hard evidence emerges. It is Rowley again who confronts us with this. 'No trace', he points out, 'of a different setting for the dialogue has survived, and it would be hard to invent anything more appropriate than what we now have. But even if our ingenuity could suggest something more appropriate, that would be no evidence that our invention was really a restoration of the original book.'[4] Still less, we might add, can we confidently disinter an *in*appropriate original (after the manner of Cheyne and others) for the author of the poem to have trimmed into the shape we know.

However much opinions differ on the compatibility of these main sections, or on the unanswerable question whether the poet composed or took over the encircling narrative, all are agreed that the prose is as masterly as the poetry. Before leaving the subject we should at least glance at N. M. Sarna's study of its form, in his article 'Epic Substratum in the Prose of Job'.[5] Sarna finds this prose 'satur-

---

[1]*From Moses to Qumran*, p.153, n.4, where Rowley quotes part of Cheyne's offering and gives references to other writers' articles. See also Gordis, *The Book of God and Man*, p.73 and notes on pp. 325f., for comments and criticisms.

[2]*Op. cit.*, p.73. The passages are Jb. 2:11–13; 42:7–10.

[3]G. Fohrer, *VT* 6 (1956), pp.249ff., esp. pp.266f.

[4]*From Moses to Qumran*, p.153.   [5]*JBL* 76 (1957), pp.13–25.

ated with poeticisms' and displaying many of the stylistic
traits which mark the Ugaritic epics: the repetitions, the
symmetry, the cumulative effects (*cf.* the arrival of messenger after messenger in 1:13ff.), the prominence of the
number seven – all of which, and more besides, indicates to
him that 'our present narrative framework is directly
derived from an ancient epic of Job'.[1]

This leaves, of course, our 'unanswerable question' still
unanswered; but to my mind Gordis has offered a reasonable
approach to it in his conclusion that the poet of the dialogue,
as a setting for his theme, 'retold a familiar story in his own
manner, keeping its principal features of style and content
unchanged'.[2]

Some problems in the poetic dialogue

1. The third round of speeches

The fact that in chapter 25 Bildad falls silent after only six
verses, and that Zophar then fails to speak at all, may
suggest rather effectively that their arguments are exhausted.[3] Yet Job's reply raises problems, partly by its unusual
length (chs. 26 – 31), but chiefly by the content of 27:7–end
(or 13–end), where he appears to speak with the very voice
of his comforters. Most commentators suspect a dislocation
of the text, by which, *e.g.*, 27:7ff. could be Zophar's missing
speech, and 26:5–end be the completion of Bildad's, to which
Job replies in 26:1–4 and 27:1–6. However, in Rowley's
words, 'the reconstructions that have been proposed are
innumerable' – of which he gives details of a mere eighteen
varieties;[4] a profusion which does nothing to strengthen the
case for such an exercise.

In defence of the text as it stands, one can maintain that
Job is making it clear that he accepts the *general* rule that
wickedness will get what it deserves, but not the friends'
insistence that there are no exceptions; still less that he
himself is reaping what he has sown. Yet, as Davidson
points out, this distinction between rule and exceptions has

---

[1]*Ibid.*, p.25. On Job as a well-known figure of antiquity, see Ezk. 14:14.
[2]*The Book of God and Man*, p.73.
[3]*Cf.* Davidson, pp.xi, 180; Andersen, p.214.
[4]*From Moses to Qumran*, p.163, n.2. Two slightly differing reconstructions are incorporated in the layout of JB and the headings of GNB (the
former without acknowledgment, the latter with marginal notes) – a
regrettable intrusion of speculation into the biblical text.

to be read into his words, for 'the language is as absolute as that of Zophar or any of the three'.[1] Other suggestions, that he is mimicking his friends in heavy irony, or that he has suddenly repented of his doubts of God's good government, require either a large assumption (since, as Dhorme observes, 'the irony . . . is in no wise apparent') or, for the latter view, a playing-down of his continuing protests (*e.g.* 30:20 ff.). A different defence of the text is offered by Andersen, who sees the whole passage, 27:7–23, as 'an imprecation, not a statement of fact', calling down on Job's false accusers the penalties of the crimes they would fasten on him (somewhat in the manner of the Israelite law against false witnesses in Dt. 19:16ff. in requital of their malice). Malice, however, would hardly be a fair charge against these three, who, for all their prejudice, had come to Job with excellent intentions.

In all, the case against the present order of the text is plausible, but weakened by its multitude of fresh proposals; while the arguments for its retention are weakened, for their part, by the necessity to read between the lines of Job's avowal in 27:7ff. For me, however, the balance is tipped towards the latter – not without misgivings – by the prior claim of a text that actually exists, over one that is no more than a choice between conjectures.

2. The Wisdom poem (ch. 28)

There is virtual unanimity on two aspects of this chapter: that it is a masterpiece, and that it stands slightly back from the immediate debate – offering the reader a reorientating respite from the strife of tongues, before Job again 'takes up his discourse' for the next three chapters. It appears to be the author's parenthesis rather than Job's, since the serenity of the passage, with its unqualified submission to the mind of God, is very different from the combative mood of Job, both before this point and after it. Job, says Davidson, 'demands knowledge. He is a chained eagle, who spreads his wings and dashes himself against the bars of his cage; he would soar unto God's place and pluck the mystery out of the darkness . . . . That he should here acquiesce in the incomprehensibility of God's way and a little further on again demand to comprehend it is very strange.'[2] What is more, if he has indeed reached this point of acquiescence, even if

[1]Davidson, p.xxxvii.   [2]Davidson, p.xxxix.

only to lapse from it again, the prolonged irony of the divine speeches will be castigating one who has already learnt his lesson once.

While few would doubt, therefore, that the poet is speaking in his own voice rather than Job's, some would question the placing of the poem here. Kaufmann, as we shall see, would make it crown the Elihu speeches, after chapter 37.[1] Gordis thinks it a youthful work of genius, found after the poet's death among the disordered leaves of the third round of speeches, but not intended for inclusion, since it 'makes the rest of the book an anticlimax' by anticipating the divine speeches.[2] One would expect Gordis therefore to transfer it to follow Job's confession, as another writer proposes,[3] but he finds no place for it, although grateful for its preservation. Plenty of scholars, however, see no objection to its present place, where, as Dhorme remarks, it can 'express a general judgment on the previous discussions' and provide for the reader 'a breathing space' after their uninterrupted flow since chapter 4, and before the long concluding speech of Job.[4] The chapter has even been compared with the chorus in a Greek tragedy, interjecting a comment on the drama.[5] While disagreeing that the work is a drama, Andersen welcomes the implication that the chapter 'sums up the case' so far; and with his strong sense of structure he observes that by echoing the language of 1:1, the final verse 'constitutes an *inclusio* which suggests that the book should be divided into Part I and Part II at this point'. Further, against the view that the chapter pre-empts the divine speeches, Andersen points out that, on the contrary, its insistence on the limitations of the human mind prepares us for the necessity of such an intervention.[6]

3. The speeches of Elihu

Gordis heads his chapter on this part of the book (Jb. 32 – 37), 'Elihu the Intruder' – and the book itself seems to bear out such an epithet, passing over him in pointed silence after he has spoken. Further, the language of this section

---

[1]See below, pp.82f.   [2]Gordis, *The Book of God and Man*, p.102.

[3]P. Szczygiel, *Das Buch Job* (1931), p.253, cited by Rowley, *From Moses to Qumran*, p.167, n.2.

[4]Dhorme, pp.li, lii, xcvii.

[5]H. Junker, *Das Buch Job* (Echter Bibel, 1951), p.54; cited in Rowley, *op. cit.*, p. 166, n.3.

[6]Andersen, pp. 223f.

sets it somewhat apart, not only by its style, more diffuse than the rest, but by some preferences in its vocabulary, and by its leanings towards Aramaic. Most scholars therefore see it as no part of the original book; but here again opinions differ over its value and its authorship. Rowley speaks for many in regarding it as adding nothing to the argument, since its view of suffering as educative has already been aired in 5:17, and the prologue has made it clear that Job's affliction was not to be explained in those terms. M. H. Pope, largely concurring with Pfeiffer, regards the Elihu speeches as the well-meaning intervention of a reader who was shocked at Job's audacity and disappointed by the failure of his friends to silence him.[1]

On the other hand, there are writers for whom these chapters are an important or even a crowning contribution to the debate. Irwin finds in Job 33 'the one real insight as yet in the book into an understanding of human woe' – referring to Elihu's constructive view of suffering in 33:14ff., and to his development of Job's mediator figure (33:23–28) into 'a gracious minister of rebuke and guidance, leading the sufferer to joyous restoration' (in which Irwin finds echoes of Ishtar's release from the underworld through the messenger of the gods).[2] More soberly, Gordis regards this material as a product of the original author, written late in life (hence the stylistic differences *and* similarities) to express a further aspect of disciplinary suffering: not merely as reproof for past sins (as in 5:17) but as part of mankind's moral education, especially against pride, the snare of the virtuous (33:17). Appreciating from 'Deutero-Isaiah' the potential fruitfulness of suffering, the poet found this 'secondary idea' worth expressing, and inserted it before the divine speeches, since it is not a conclusion but a supplement. It is not the whole truth: '. . . the whole truth is not with man, but with God.'[3]

Another scholar who sees Elihu as a mouthpiece of the poet himself is Kaufmann, in whose view the burning question here is the defence of God's moral providence against Job's questionings. In proof of it, Elihu points to divine

---

[1]Pope, p.xxvi; *cf.* R. H. Pfeiffer, *Introduction to the Old Testament* (A. & C. Black, 1952), p.673. For a longer list, see Rowley, *From Moses to Qumran*, p.148, n.2.

[2]Irwin, on Jb. 33 (and on chs. 14, 16 and 19) in *Peake's Commentary*. He assigns the remaining Elihu speeches to three further (and inferior) authors.

[3]Gordis, *The Book of God and Man*, pp. 113–116.

chastenings and judgments, both personal (33:14–33) and
political (34:16–37); to his preservation of the earth and its
inhabitants (34:13–15), and finally, in chapter 28 (which
Kaufmann would make the climax of Elihu's speech), his
gift of true wisdom.[1]

An unusual point is made by Andersen, that Elihu's role
in the book is that of an adjudicator, not a protagonist. 'He is
the first of two who record their impressions of what has
been said in chapters 3 – 31. Elihu gives the human
estimate; Yahweh gives the divine appraisal. There is no
need for the Lord to comment also on Elihu's summing up;
His silence on this point is no more a problem than the
absence of any final show-down with the Satan at the end.'[2]

For a longer list of writers and opinions on this section,
see Rowley's extensive footnotes in *From Moses to Qumran*,
pp. 147–150.

4. The second divine speech (40:6 – 41:34)

While only a few critics have rejected *both* of the divine
speeches, many take exception to the second, regarding it as
poetically inferior to the first.[3] They find it laboured and
exaggerated in its description, in contrast to the rapid
sketches of chs. 38 – 39; exotic in its choice of two non-
Palestinian monsters for its subjects; and superfluous in
view of Job's surrender before it has begun.

Most of these objections are either aesthetic or arbitrary,
and can be countered by opposite judgments from scholars of
equal competence. Even to set them out is (one may feel) to
expose the majority of them as quibbles to support the only
serious charge: that the first speech has already achieved its
object. To this charge Gordis has replied that the second
speech, so far from labouring the points already made,
'represents a higher level in the argument, an ascent from
God's creative power as manifested in creatures that are
independent of man, to God's creative joy in creatures that
are positively dangerous and repugnant to man'.[4] And on
Job's two stages of response, which some would telescope

[1]Y. Kaufmann, *The Religion of Israel* (Chicago, 1960), pp.334–338.

[2]Andersen, p.51.

[3]Rowley claims the support of Ewald, Dillmann, Cheyne, Gray, Eissfeldt
'and many others', in this rejection; but mentions Lefèvre, Hertzberg, Lods,
Skehan and Gordis among those who retain both speeches (*The Book of Job*,
p.15).

[4]Gordis, *The Book of God and Man*, p.123. *Cf.* Dhorme, p.xcv.

into one, he makes the perceptive remark that 'Job's first answer strikes the note of submission and silence; it is only in the second that he attains a measure of repentance and acceptance. Job is convinced by God's words, but not easily: two stages are required for the argument'.[1]

Moreover, as Davidson for one has pointed out, it is God's second speech which calls on Job to deck himself with majesty and set the world to rights (40:10–14) – thus reminding him '*first*, that omnipotence is necessary in the ruler of all; and *second*, that rule of the world consists in keeping in check the forces of evil'.[2] Then, to bring home to him not crushingly but provocatively, vividly, his unfitness to call God to order, he is invited to try his hand on two of his fellow creatures, 'which I made as I made you' (40:15). The exuberance and hyperbole of their descriptions, which some writers have disdained, can be assessed on the contrary as providing 'a terrific climax'[3] – one which evokes from Job a spontaneous cry of admiration, 'so different from the reserve of his reply to the first speech . . .:

> "You can do everything!
> None of your plans can be frustrated!" '[4]

Is there even a disarming note in the divine challenge to Job to try his hand at world government (40:10–14)? To Gordis it is the climax of the divine irony, 'infinitely keen yet infinitely kind . . . . Here on the one hand is God's moving acknowledgment that the world order is not perfect, and on the other, an affirmation of the complexity of the universe and of the conflicting interests which divine concern must encompass and reconcile. . . . Thus God has conceded that there are flaws in His creation, and evils which He has not conquered . . .'[5]

If Gordis implies by this a divine confession of defeat, it would be at variance not only with the rest of Scripture but with the robust tone of what precedes and follows these five verses (indeed, on the face of it, with the tone of the verses themselves). Yet he is surely right to emphasize God's frank avowal of the present state of things *in his forbearance* – an avowal which could prompt Job to reflect that, after all, the Omnipotent knows what he is permitting, and why, and for how long.

---

[1] Gordis, *ibid.*   [2] Davidson, p. 279.
[3] Andersen, p. 291; *cf.* Dhorme, pp. xciv f.
[4] Andersen, *ibid.*   [5] Gordis, p. 119.

If it raises such questions, however indirectly, the second divine speech can hardly be thought superfluous, nor Job's response to it a mere reiteration of his brief disclaimer at 40:4–5.

The overall purpose of the book

At first sight it may seem obvious that the concern of this book is to throw decisive light on the problem of suffering, or, more broadly, on God's principles of government. But its refusal 'to justify God's ways to man', and the hearing that it gives to many voices, also the diversity of interpretations which have been offered, should warn us against defining its objectives too narrowly. Among its major topics, it probes (to quote one survey) into 'disinterested obedience, . . . innocent suffering, social oppression, religious experience and pious duty, a man's relation to God, and the nature of that God'[1] – and that list could be extended to include the nature of wisdom, and the finality of death.

To some commentators this many-sidedness is compounded by multiple authorship and divergent outlooks in the making of the book. W. A. Irwin, for example, while finding 'high interest and great worth' in every part of Job,[2] sees the poetic dialogue (short of 28–31) as the original work, whose point is missed by the additional sections (except, to some extent, the Elihu material[3]), and indeed 'nullified' by the divine speeches. The crucial theme, as he sees it, is the gradual recognition of Job that death is in some way a 'transition, through which, having been tested, one comes out like purified gold',[4] through the aid of the 'intermediary' – the longed-for arbitrator (9:33), witness (16:19) and redeemer (19:25). In all this, Irwin sees an indebtedness to the myths of dying and rising deities, through which the poet sees that suffering is not a product of our disordered state but 'is in the nature of things – God himself suffers'. He glimpses the almost Pauline concept that here is our highest means of fellowship with God. Such, for Irwin, is 'the ultimate answer which the Dialogue offers . . .'.[5]

Another angle on the theme of death and resurrection is the notion of a ritualized dying and rising of the king, as seen by some interpreters of the Psalms. M.Bič,[6] in an

---

[1]A. and M. Hanson, *Job*, p.15.   [2]*Peake's Commentary*, section 339 f.
[3]See above, p.82.   [4]*Peake's Commentary*, section 355 i.
[5]*Ibid.*, section 356 c, d.
[6]'Le juste et l'impie dans le livre de Job', *VTS* 15 (1966), pp. 33–43.

article in 1966, seized on some verbal affinities between the laments of Job and those of the Davidic king in the first book of the Psalter, to suggest that this sufferer too is kingly. Moreover Job's ordeal is vicarious, since he intercedes for his friends. Like the humiliated king, he is rescued by God, and the story is therefore not about theodicy but about the conflict between God's kingdom and its enemies (represented by Job's comforters, whose wisdom is of this world and whose origins are from Edom, the traditional foe). Job, as the righteous and quasi-kingly sufferer and intercessor, foreshadows Christ and his redemptive passion.

Both of these approaches, while they look for truths expounded elsewhere in the Bible, read more into the book of Job than can be properly read out of it (although Irwin is at pains to deny this), and make much of verbal coincidences with other writings. Bič, for example, enlists the very taunt of Eliphaz in 15:7ff., 'Are you the first man that was born? . . . Have you listened in the council of God?', to invest Job with the supposed attributes of the primal man simply by using such expressions. Irwin, for his part, seizes on Job's phrase for death as 'the way whence I shall not return', as an echo of Ishtar's formula, 'the land of no return' (Jb.16:22; *ANET*, p.107a), and is impressed by the verbal similarity between the cry, 'I know that my Redeemer lives', and, 'So I knew that alive was Puissant Baal' (Jb.19:25; *ANET*, p.140b). These and similar wisps of material surely advertise their insufficiency, however ingeniously they are put together.

S. Terrien shares Irwin's impression that the Redeemer saying echoes the Baal Epic, although he is more tentative than Irwin over attributing Job's yearning for a heavenly mediator, or the poet's theology of suffering, to pagan stories of the gods. Indeed his overall view of Job's experience is put in terms strongly coloured by the New Testament, since (as he puts it) the poet 'understood almost as well as Paul that righteousness is not the work of man but remains always the gift of God. The book of Job . . . leads straight to the New Testament'.[1] In another passage he can put it that 'travelling into the theological unknown, he was led unwittingly to imply the necessity of a Christ, learned the sufficiency of grace, and was brought to the threshold of pure religion'.[2] So the book is not a theodicy – for man cannot

---

[1] *Job (Commentaire de l'Ancien Testament*, 13), p.49.
[2] *The Interpreter's Bible*, 3, p.897b.

arrogate to himself the right to justify God without deifying himself.[1] It is the story of a spiritual pilgrimage, in which Job is set free from the prison of himself and of his imagined rights, to be 'saved at the moment of his surrender'; and to find, through God's coming to him, what he had not found through tradition or through moralizing.[2]

Along very similar lines, Harold Knight argued that Job's very success as a righteous man and a philanthropist had imprisoned him in a moralistic and man-centred theology, until disaster had opened his eyes to the extent of human suffering and had brought him into an overwhelming encounter with God. The implied message of the book was that *Israel* likewise needed such a liberation. Too pre-occupied, like Job, with questions of ethics and of her destiny, she needed to be renewed by spiritual, mystical communion with the God whom she had tried to confine within a theological system.[3]

A radical rejoinder to all such emphases on mystical or existential encounter at the expense of explicit theology was made by M. Tsevat in an article, 'The Meaning of the Book of Job',[4] where he argued that if the subject debated by Job with his friends was the suffering of the innocent, we should expect the *content* of God's reply, not the mere fact of it, to resolve the matter. If that content was no more than a reminder of the complexity of God's world, this was mere 'education through overwhelming', and it evaded the issue. Or if, as Martin Buber has claimed, God's speech demonstrates that divine justice is freer and more creative than human retributive justice – bestowing, instead, on each creature what is uniquely appropriate to it – then this too is no answer; for the question remains, why is it *appropriate* for the innocent to suffer? Tsevat is equally dismissive of Gordis's emphasis on the reassuring beauty of God's creation, as revealed in the divine speeches – a mere anodyne, he considers, rather than an answer. Nor can he fully agree with Fohrer that the issue is not 'why do the righteous suffer?' but '*how* should they suffer?' – to which the answer in that case would come not in the divine speeches but in the final response of Job.

Tsevat's thesis is that God is destroying Job's assumption that justice is the moral cornerstone of the universe. It is

---

[1]*Job*, p.48.   [2]*The Interpreter's Bible*, 3, p.902a; *cf. Job*, p.47.
[3]H. Knight, *SJT* 9 (1956), pp. 63–76.
[4]*HUCA* 37 (1966), pp.73–106, reprinted in *SAIW*, pp.341–374.

only *man's* obligation, in man's affairs: not God's in his –
though it is an option open to him.[1] For besides justice and
injustice there is, he claims, a third concept: 'nonjustice'. 'He
who speaks to man in the Book of Job is neither a just nor an
unjust god but God.'[2] So the book 'does more than demyth-
ologize the world: it also "de-moralizes" it, which is to say,
makes it amoral' – but thereby opens the way to a loftier,
because purely disinterested, religion and morality. 'If you
decide to do what is good,' it implies, 'do it because it is
good.'[3]

In the process, however, of praising goodness for its own
sake, and of stressing the denial in the book of Job that a
man's fortunes are to be construed as his deserts, Tsevat has
slipped into cutting the knot of the problem – making the
author of Job ease the tension between ultimate justice and
present experience by 'shattering' (as Tsevat admits) 'a
central biblical doctrine'.[4] The amoral God he discovers here
is one whose thoughts and ways are not simply higher than
ours, but alien to them and to his plainest words.

It is truer both to the rest of Scripture and to the meaning
of fellowship between God and man, to see the divine
speeches not (with Tsevat) as narrowing the scope of justice,
nor (with some existentialists) as by-passing the mind, but
as enlarging Job's thinking and his faith together. This,
incidentally, is the thrust of Gordis's exposition of them,
which Tsevat took to mean merely that as you steep yourself
in the beauty of the creation your pain is assuaged. Gordis's
point, shared by many others, is rather that the reminder to
Job of mystery, beauty and harmony in the natural world
invites the inference that the equally baffling moral order is
no less glorious, and can be rejoiced in with no less con-
fidence.

This, expressed in various ways, is probably the widest
consensus on the final message of the book. To it, almost as
many individual nuances are added as there are writers who
share this general view – whether one listens to Dhorme, for
instance, who points out, further, the impetus given by the
book of Job to the shift of emphasis in intertestamental
literature, and on into the New Testament, from present to
future retribution;[5] or to Rowley, whose remarks on suffering as potentially an honour are quoted above on page

---

[1]*HUCA*, p.104; *SAIW*, p.372.   [2]*HUCA*, p.105; *SAIW*, p.373.
[3]*HUCA*, p.102; *cf.* p.104. *SAIW*, p.370; *cf.* p.372.
[4]*HUCA*, p.103; *SAIW*, p.371.   [5]Dhorme, p.cli.

58; or to Pope, who is sensitive to the struggle involved in any journey from despair to trust, and who believes that 'the transition from fear and hatred to trust and even love of this One – from God the Enemy to God the Friend and Companion – is the pilgrimage of every man of faith';[1] or again, to Andersen who sees (but more soberly than Bič – above, pp.85f.) in 'the passion of Job . . . an early sketch of the greatest Sufferer. . . . What Job longed for blindly has actually happened. God Himself has joined us in our hell of loneliness . . . . (Here) is the final answer to Job and to all the Jobs of humanity'.[2]

[1]Pope, p.lxxvii.   [2]Andersen, pp. 72f.

6

Ecclesiastes
A life worth living?

The audacity of Job in face of the anomalies of life is matched and even outmatched here – for now the question is whether life itself has any point. With no Job-like prologue to let us into any secrets, no dialogue to balance one point of view against another, and no answering voice from heaven, we take the full force of the opening salvo, 'Vanity of vanities . . . ! All is vanity', and finally receive it again as Qoheleth's[1] parting shot (12:8).[2] But while the word 'vanity'[3] is heard more than thirty times in these twelve chapters, and finds echoes of its dark mood in such a cry as 'Who knows what is good for man?' (6:12) or, more desperately, 'I thought the dead . . . more fortunate than the living' – and the stillborn more fortunate than either (4:2–3; 6:3b–5), this is not the whole story. There are enough crosscurrents of joy and of orthodox wisdom and piety to make the overall intention of the book a question not easily settled.

Since answers to that question are almost as numerous as the scholars who have wrestled with it, I have given a

[1]This word, usually translated 'the Preacher', is from the same root as *qāhāl*, 'assembly', 'congregation', and implies an office-bearer, perhaps one who summoned the faithful for instruction. Crenshaw (*Old Testament Wisdom*, p.148) tentatively suggests a gatherer of data about life; but it is doubtful whether such a process could be rightly called summoning. The word is used both as a name and (12:8) as a title. A glimpse of Qoheleth at work is given in 12:9–10.

[2]Beyond reasonable doubt the remaining verses, 12:9–14, with their portrait of the writer, their warning against unauthorized teachings and their summary of the discourse, are an editorial epilogue or epilogues.

[3]Heb. *hebel*, a mere breath, a vapour, *i.e.* transience, emptiness; hence futility.

separate chapter to a survey – far from complete – of the debate (pp. 105–115). The present chapter looks at two alternative ways of trying to do justice to the tensions in the book without ascribing them to the intervention of correctors or supplementers. The first of these alternatives is to read the book as Qoheleth's debate with himself, torn between what he cannot help seeing and what he still cannot help believing. The second is to see it as his challenge to the man of the world to think his own position through to its bitter end, with a view to seeking something less futile. After looking at these two approaches – not the only two that are possible – the chapter will group together some of the main subjects explored by Qoheleth, and suggest how they lead towards 'the end of the matter' as defined by the epilogue.

First interpretation

The book as Qoheleth's debate with himself

'As I mused, the fire burned; then I spoke . . . .' That fragment from Psalm 39:3, a poem about man as *hebel*, 'vanity' or 'a mere breath',[1] might almost be Qoheleth's own confession, if his book is to be taken as the broodings and outbursts of a man of many moods and total honesty, whose faith is hard pressed by the seeming futility of existence. To him the clouds, so to speak, chase each other across a sky which seldom clears for more than a moment. The darkest of them we have already mentioned, in speaking of *hebel*, vanity, and the deep misgivings which go with such a word.

At intervals, some light breaks through as he commends enjoyment of God's uncomplicated gifts. Yet even this is clouded, however lightly, with reminders that all such joys are fleeting, however beautiful in their time. One of the most festive of these passages is also the most brutally outspoken – and a recent version spares us nothing of it:

Go ahead – eat your food and be happy; drink your wine and be cheerful. It's all right with God. Always look happy and cheerful. Enjoy life with the woman you love, as long as you live the useless life that God has given you in this world. Enjoy every useless day of it, because that is all you will get for all your trouble. Work hard at whatever you do, because there will be no action, no thought, no know-

[1]Ps. 39:11 (12, Heb.)

ledge, no wisdom in the world of the dead – and that is where you are going (Ec. 9:7–10, GNB).

Much more rarely, and flanked by some of the most sombre thoughts, a saying will suddenly shine out with perfect orthodoxy:

> I said in my heart, God will judge the righteous and the wicked, for he has appointed a time for every matter, and for every work (3:17).

> Though a sinner does evil a hundred times and prolongs his life, yet I know that it will be well with those who fear God, because they fear before him; but it will not be well with the wicked, neither will he prolong his days like a shadow, because he does not fear before God (8:12–13).

> Rejoice, O young man, in your youth . . . ; walk in the ways of your heart and the sight of your eyes. But know that for all these things God will bring you into judgment (11:9).

It is possible to interpret even these passages as no more than reminders that all men alike are under sentence of physical death, and that (despite some exceptions) sin tends to hasten that sentence. It is, alternatively, tempting to treat these sudden affirmations, taken at their face value, as well-meaning insertions by subsequent correctors. Both these views will be discussed in the next chapter, along with yet others. But it is worth taking seriously the hypothesis that the entire book faithfully reflects the groaning and travailing of an exceptional mind: one which scorns to present a case which leaves out anything that would threaten it. On this view, Qoheleth (not unlike Job) is tortured by each fresh evidence of futility and tragedy, and indeed twists the knife in his own wound, yet cannot in honesty renounce his basic faith. It is this very clash of convictions that gives the cry of 'Vanity' its poignancy – for why should transience trouble us if we have no more inkling of eternity than have the beasts?

It would be pleasing to find Qoheleth's darkest thoughts eventually dispersing; but instead, his preoccupations can only alternate, and unequally at that. The clouds return after the rain, and in 12:8 his words end as they began, with 'Vanity of vanities . . . ; all is vanity'. Yet light is stronger than darkness, and the shafts of it which have broken through at 3:17, *etc.* (see above) are enough to promise its eventual and total triumph. Therefore the summarizer of the book is doing no violence to the argument when at 12:13–14 he picks out Qoheleth's rare interjections of faith as the true conclusion of his search. For if God is there, and if one has already dared to say, 'I know that it will be well with those who fear God . . .' (8:12), there is nothing that can trump that card. *There can be no other 'end of the matter'.*

To see Ecclesiastes, then, as the record – almost the diary – of the author's debate with himself, is one approach which allows us to grapple with the book as it stands, unexpurgated; and it does justice to the writer's predominantly sombre mood.

I am drawn, however, to a second interpretation which equally respects the integrity of the book, but sees it as a searching criticism of human self-sufficiency.[1]

Second interpretation

The book as Qoheleth's challenge to the secularist

G. S. Hendry has expressed this view as follows:

Qoheleth writes from concealed premises, and his book is in reality a major work of apologetic or 'eristic' theology. Its apparent worldliness is dictated by its aim: Qoheleth is addressing the general public whose view is bounded by the horizons of this world; he meets them on their own ground, and proceeds to convict them of its inherent vanity. . . . His book is in fact a critique of secularism and of secularized religion.[2]

Looked at in this way, the shafts of light that we have noticed are signals to the reader that the author's own position and conclusions are very different from those of the secularist, in whose shoes he is standing for the purpose of his thesis. Without these signals and their final confirmation (12:13–14) the book would simply preach despair, or at best a mere whistling in the dark. But with them, it is saying that the abyss of final vanity is the destination of

[1]I pursue this at greater length in *A time to mourn, and a time to dance*: Ecclesiastes and the way of the world (IVP, 1976); reissued as *The Message of Ecclesiastes* (IVP, 1984). See also M. A. Eaton's closely argued Tyndale Commentary, *Ecclesiastes* (IVP, 1983).

[2]G. S. Hendry, article 'Ecclesiastes' in the *New Bible Commentary* (Third Edition, IVP, 1970), p.570.

every road *but one*. Qoheleth can therefore be relentless in facing that final emptiness, first because it is the truth about this passing world, but also because there is a bigger truth to live by.

So throughout the book, with the rarest of disclaimers, he shocks us into seeing life and death strictly from ground level, and into reaching the only conclusions from that standpoint that honesty will allow. Yet he is leading rather than driving us. As a real citizen of this tantalizing world, he feels acutely the futility that he describes. He burns at the injustices and disappointments of life, and mourns the passing of youth and the universality of death – even while he bids us set our hearts not on earthly vanities themselves but on our Creator, from whom we can gladly, responsibly, accept them for what they are, but in whom alone is the 'eternity', the 'for ever' (3:11,14) of which he has made us conscious.

The survey of the book's contents, which follows, will reflect something of this approach.

The subject-matter

While any framework must sit ill on this book of ever-shifting patterns and preoccupations, we can at least group together for convenience some of its main concerns. The following is a suggestion for a working model.

A. Truths about God

1. Creator
2. Disposer
3. Unsearchable
4. Judge of all
5. To be reverenced and obeyed

B. Truths about life

1. Pointers to despair:
   a. the ceaseless round
   b. the fruitless search
   c. the elusive pattern
   d. the unmanageable: misrule, mischance, death
2. Mitigations:
   a. simple joys
   b. common sense
   c. enterprise

3. The point of rest:
God, whose service is man's *raison d'être*,
whose judgment leaves nothing without meaning

A. Truths about God

Although Qoheleth is attacking the secularist outlook, he does not have to reckon with theoretical atheism: only with a thoughtless attitude towards a God whose existence is unquestioned but unappreciated. God is presented here as:

1. Creator

This strong word, used in the Old Testament of God alone, occurs here only once (12:1); but Ecclesiastes, in common with the rest of the Old Testament, grounds all existence in God, who 'makes everything', who begins and ends every life (11:5; 12:7), who appoints for everything its proper season (3:11), and who made man upright in the beginning (7:29) – who therefore cannot be blamed for man's perversity.[1]

2. Disposer

When Paul said that 'the creation was subjected to vanity . . . by reason of him who subjected it, in hope' (Rom. 8:20, RV), he could well have had Ecclesiastes in mind (adding only the important thrust of his last two words), since the 'unhappy business' of 'vanity and a striving after wind' is seen in this book as what '*God has given* to the sons of men to be busy with' (1:13). If that is his general ordinance, he also deals out individual fortunes exactly as he chooses (*e.g.* 2:24–26). Life's ironies as well as its delights are from his hand (*e.g.* the gift of material success without the power to enjoy it, 6:2); and there is no arguing with what he decides to do – for we must be taught our place. 'God has made it so, in order that men should fear before him' (3:14). So,

In the day of prosperity be joyful, and in the day of adversity consider; God has made the one as well as the other, so that man may not find out anything that will be after him (7:14).

This leads us to the next emphasis, that God is:

---

[1] Contrast the 'Babylonian Theodicy', line 280, 'With lies, and not truth, they [*sc.* the gods] endowed them forever.' See below, p.137.

3. Unsearchable

This does not preclude his power to reveal himself (*cf.* the description of true worship as 'to draw near *to listen*', 5:1), but it silences the theological wiseacre. Man has an inkling of God's activity, but no grasp of it 'from the beginning to the end' (3:11).

> That which is, is far off, and deep, very deep; who can find it out? (7:24; *cf.* 8:17).

More seriously still, there is no way of even telling whether, as we would put it, the universe is friendly or hostile. Are we to go by its glories or its terrors? But Qoheleth is too realistic to speak of anything as secondary as the universe. His question is about God, in whose hands we find ourselves; and he defies us to arrive at an answer:

> whether it is love or hate man does not know (9:1).

Yet the fact that for Qoheleth there is a sharp distinction between what can be learnt of God from observation and what can be affirmed by faith, emerges clearly in what follows:

4. Judge of all

This is double-edged. It has its terror for the wicked (8:13) and its warning for the exuberant (11:9), and there are moments when it could be simply reminding us that all things alike are under a death sentence (3:17 ff.). But in the context of life's injustices and apparent lack of meaning, the fact that justice will at last be done (8:10–13; 12:14) is not bad news but good. As I have remarked elsewhere, in Ecclesiastes we have faced 'the appalling inference that nothing has meaning, nothing matters under the sun. It is then that we can hear, as the good news which it is, that *everything* matters – "for God will bring every deed into judgment . . ." '.[1]

5. To be reverenced

The 'fear' of God carries here both aspects of that expression: both the chastened reticence enjoined in the 'Guard your

---

[1]*The Message of Ecclesiastes*, p.20.

steps' passage (5:1–7) and the humble responsiveness implied not only in the summary, 'Fear God, and keep his commandments' (12:13), but also in the placing of 3:14b ('that men should fear before him') in the context of God's wise, generous and self-consistent will (3:10–15). Both emphases are necessary if Qoheleth is to heal us as well as smite us.

B. Truths about life

Partly consecutively (in the sequence of the first three chapters and in the movement of the last two towards the conclusion), but more often with sporadic thrusts at one aspect or another, the treatment of the facts of life will focus on some pointers to despair, some mitigating factors, and the one point of rest.

1. Pointers to despair

a. The ceaseless round
This is the analogy drawn in 1:2–11 between the restless circularity of nature and that of human history. It is not the strictly cyclic view of, *e.g.*, Stoicism, whereby the whole sequence of events throughout the age will come round again in the next age and the next, for ever. But it sees the generations rising and falling to no apparent purpose; each toiling for what cannot last or satisfy, eventually to fade even from memory.

b. The fruitless search
In 1:12 – 2:11 (or 24) Qoheleth dons the mantle of Solomon – or rather, of a super-Solomon, for he pictures himself as a king who has surpassed all who were before him in Jerusalem (2:9) – in order to explore the limits of what life might offer to the ideally gifted and advantaged. From this perspective he examines the rewards of reason and (here is a modern touch) of unreason; of pleasure both sensual and aesthetic; of creative enterprises; the satisfactions of the connoisseur and the collector; even of the activist (2:10b) who enjoys hard work for its own sake. He distinguishes between them –

I saw that wisdom excels folly as light excels darkness (2:13)

97

– but finds in that very fact a crowning frustration, since death will level all distinctions. His hunger for something that will last, this missing element of 'for ever', of which God has made man conscious (as the great statement of 3:11 will declare) is already expressed in 2:16–17:

> For of the wise man as of the fool there is no enduring[1] remembrance . . . So I hated life . . . ; for all is vanity and a striving after wind.

c. The elusive pattern

The beguiling rhythm in 3:1–8, of a time for this and a time for that, rocks us awake, in the end, rather than asleep, with the question,

> What gain has the worker from his toil? (3:9)

– for it is evident that we spend our days shuttling back and forth in a pattern that we can neither choose nor fully grasp, busy now with one thing, now with its opposite. Our chances of seizing the right moment, or reaching a goal, or securing what we gain, are riddled with this uncertainty. It is made all the more tantalizing by the brief flowerings of beauty in the world, which, like all else, have only their appointed moments, and by our disturbing ability to compare the fleeting with the idea of the eternal.

> I have seen the business that God has given to the sons of men to be busy with. He has made everything beautiful in its time; also he has put eternity into man's mind, yet so that he cannot find out what God has done from the beginning to the end (3:10–11).

Qoheleth admittedly would not have us be downcast by these reflections, but aware of our transience, grateful for our blessings (12–13) and humble before the one whose grasp, unlike ours, reaches from first to last, and of whose work nothing is lost.

> I know that whatever God does endures for ever; . . . God has made it so, in order that men should fear before him (3:14).

This, together with Qoheleth's prescience of a judgment that will override our travesties of justice (3:16–17), is one of the rare glimpses he allows us of the answer to despair: the answer of 'eternity' to 'vanity'. It is only man in his self-

---

[1]Heb. *lᵉʿôlām*, 'for ever'; *cf.* 3:11,14.

sufficiency who should be disquieted by this study of life as inexorably time-conditioned.

d. *The unmanageable: misrule, mischance and death*

Misrule is a recurrent grief of Qoheleth, to which he reacts at one moment with conviction of a future judgment (3:16–17; 8:10–13), but at another with plain anguish for the tears of the oppressed (4:1–3), and a sense of helplessness in face of towering bureaucracy (5:8) and all degrees of tyranny where 'man lords it over man to his hurt' (8:9). The picture is not uniformly dark. Kings and officials have their uses (5:9), and some of them their virtues (10:17); but nothing is certain at this level, and a land may find itself at any moment in the hands of fools and upstarts, the weak and the debauched (10:5–6,16). This political uncertainty is only one aspect of, secondly,

Mischance – from which no area of life is free. The point is put most forcefully at 9:11–12:

> Again I saw that under the sun the race is not to the swift, nor the battle to the strong, nor bread to the wise . . . ; but time and chance happen to them all. For man does not know his time . . . .'

Elsewhere, too, this is borne in on us by examples of 'riches . . . lost in a bad venture' (5:14), or amassed but not enjoyed (6:2); and of life's unpredictable awards to vice and virtue (8:14). All this, we are told, is God's rebuke to our cocksureness:

> When things go well, be glad; but when things go ill, consider this: God has set the one alongside the other in such a way that no one can find out what is to happen next (7:14, NEB).

In one realm, however, what makes life unmanageable is not its unpredictability but its one certainty: that is, thirdly,

Death. No-one has faced this more resolutely than Qoheleth. It was this that gave him second thoughts over his praise of wisdom, 'seeing that in the days to come all will have been long forgotten' (2:16 [13–17]). After this reflection, whatever subject he touches has to face this test and be found wanting. Whatever may be the successes of a man's best years, the entirety of his career has to be mapped as a journey from a naked beginning to a naked end (5:15).

Just as he came, so shall he go; and what gain has he that
he toiled for the wind . . . ? (5:16).

As J. S. Whale put it in a notable Cambridge Lecture, 'If
death means that all is over and there is nothing more, it is
life which is pervaded with tragic irrationality. Every col-
umn in the great human tot-book adds up to precisely the
same result, Zero.'[1]

2. Mitigations

a. Simple joys
This theme returns so often[2] that to many writers it is here,
rather than in the fear of God, that Qoheleth finds fulfilment
of a sort (an opinion not shared by Qoheleth's editor: 12:13).
It is typical of his honesty that he gives full value to this
sweetening of life, for all his insistence on the bitterness of
death. Two turns of speech, however, keep reminding us
that these modest pleasures are not goals to live for, but
bonuses or consolations to be gratefully accepted. First, they
are 'from the hand of God', and to be taken as such with a
clear conscience ('for God has already approved what you
do', 9:7; *i.e.*, as the author of these joys he has shown his
pleasure in them). This is very different from a defiant
hedonism.[3] Secondly – and this is the other 'constant' in
Qoheleth's thought – these joys, however innocent, are passing, like all else that is 'under the sun'. So they too are
subject to 'vanity'. There can be no pretence that they are
more than palliatives, brightening 'the few days of (one's)
life', the 'vain life which he has given you under the sun'
(5:18; 9:9). And in the last of all these passages the invitation is coupled with a reminder of not only vanity but
judgment:

Rejoice, O young man, in your youth; . . . walk in the ways
of your heart and the sight of your eyes. But know that for
all these things God will bring you into judgment. Remove
vexation from your mind, and put away pain from your

[1]*Christian Doctrine* (C.U.P., 1941), p.173. (My italics.)
[2]See 2:24–26; 3:12–13,22; 5:18–20; 8:15; 9:7–10; 11:7–10.
[3]Indeed it can be argued that with the first of these passages (2:24) we
reach 'a turning-point in the argument. . . . Having exposed the bankruptcy
of our pretended autonomy, the Preacher now points to the God who
occupies the heavenly realm, and to the life of faith in him' (M. A. Eaton,
Ecclesiastes, p.73).

body; for youth and the dawn of life are vanity (11:9–10).

Yet this, like the exhortations to receive joy as God-given, is to *enhance* its value, not to diminish it. Under that appraising eye it will have reason to be pure, not corrupt; and it will know something more than triviality and 'the laughter of fools'.

A second way in which Qoheleth rallies us from mere defeatism is one which links him to the everyday wisdom of Proverbs. Much, he points out, can be mitigated through:

b. Common sense

His warnings against overrating the world's temporary structures are far from invitations to despise them, and his shock-treatment of conventional wisdom is not a root-and-branch rejection of it.

True, the shocks that he administers can be very sharp. The opening sayings of chapter 7 still take us by surprise; for just as we are nodding agreement with the valuable remark of 7:1a,

> A good name is better than precious ointment,

we are 'thrown' by its companion line:

> and the day of death, than the day of birth.

This is followed by more in the same vein; but as the chapter proceeds, its aphorisms grow less paradoxical. Like those of chapter 10, most of them would be quite at home in the book of Proverbs, although to some extent this reassuring material is being used, no doubt, to enhance the impact of the unexpected.[1] But the common-sense sayings are too numerous to be simply foils for the occasional paradox or dark thought. Their role is positive and bracing: to show that there is much that can be done by plain good sense, since all too many of our troubles are of our own making. Just as the brevity of life is no reason to reject its joys (as we have seen), so its blows and hazards are no argument against using our intelligence to mitigate them. The only proviso is that we treat this *as* a mitigation, not an answer. The deeper questions remain. Meanwhile Qoheleth has a third practicality to recommend:

c. Enterprise

He begins his final advice (11:1–6) by turning the argument

[1]See further, pp.109f., 122f., below.

from life's uncertainty upside down. He faces the fact of it as squarely as ever, repeating '*you know not*' four times in six verses, but he treats it as a call to action: a compelling reason to spread one's ventures and redouble one's efforts. If our very existence is a mystery – we did not have to solve it to be created or to procreate! (5) – we need not be paralysed by the lesser things we cannot know or alter: only be reminded of what does lie within reach, in the context of what is known only to God 'who makes everything'. The implications of that last phrase are not drawn out, but it begins to prepare us for the summons of 12:1 at the climax of the book: to remember our Creator while we still have all our faculties about us.

For in 11:7–10 not only the uncertainties of life but now its only certainty – death – is treated as a spur to lively and positive response. All that was said before about accepting simple joys is reaffirmed and heightened; but so too is the reminder that these good things cannot last – with the added warning (quoted above, p.100) that they cannot be abused with impunity. These joys, then, are provisional, even double-edged. Yet the very mention of God's judgment on the handling of them, and thereby his assessment of one's life, brings the hint of an exception to the vanity of all things. To be sure, what God finally condemns can have no other name than vanity; but what he finally approves cannot be held in anything but honour. In that possible approval there is at last something, indeed everything, to live for. The remaining chapter, which flows straight on from this,[1] urges us to make this and nothing less our aim.

3. The point of rest

The call that opens the last chapter – 'Remember your Creator' – brings us at once and without elaboration to the end of the search. In contrast to the uncertain values and self-absorption of the early chapters, here is absorption with the One whose right to it is absolute and whose judgment (11:9) is final. Above the frustrations of 'time and chance', whatever he does endures for ever (3:14). And since the opportunity to respond to him is fleeting, and the only time at our disposal is the present, Qoheleth devotes his most haunting eloquence to the reader's prospect of decay and death. His last words, 'Vanity of vanities ...' (12:8), re-

[1]12:1 reads literally, 'And remember...'

inforce the body-blow that had opened his attack (1:2).

Two questions, if not three, arise here. First, do Qoheleth's own words end with verse 8? The way they echo his opening cry suggests this strongly, and the commending of his work to the reader in verses 9–12 has the sound of a new voice (compare verse 10 with Jn. 21:24b). The remaining verses are no less authoritative, as canonical Scripture, for that.

Secondly, does 'Vanity of vanities' cancel the positive thrust of 'Remember your Creator' and the equally positive 'end of the matter' in verses 13–14? To answer this we should notice that such a sequence is typical of Qoheleth's overall method, which is to present a prevailing picture of earthly futility and tragedy, almost (*yet not wholly*) unrelieved by any glimmer of light. Where other writers would commend the light to us directly, Qoheleth does it *by making the darkness intolerable*, allowing the light only the rarest gleam to provoke the observant into second thoughts. 'Remember your Creator' is, apart from the clear daylight of the epilogue, the last of these moments before the clouds close in again; and on this occasion Qoheleth is explicit in his warning that they will indeed close in, and in his appeal for right relationship with God before they do.

But this leads to the third question, namely what answer even such a relationship can give to a prospect of universal death. Qoheleth, by insisting that God is judge of every act (8:11–13) and every man (3:17), brings eternity to bear on us, even though time, without that dimension, destroys us. It follows that nothing is meaningless, for God assesses it; and no-one is forgotten, however short may be the human memory.

This is exceedingly far-reaching. Nothing less than this can answer the nihilism, the 'vanity of vanities', with which Qoheleth faithfully confronts the merely earthbound. If every act, every person, matters to the eternal God, man can play his part in earnest. Nothing will go unregarded, unremembered or unvalued. But beyond this Qoheleth will not venture. To the question whether human death has any different sequel from that of animals his answer is, 'Who knows?' (3:21), and this must control the meaning we assign to 12:7, 'the spirit returns to God who gave it'. As in Psalm 104:29–30, it will speak only of the breath, or spirit (*rûaḥ*, as here), which God lends to man and beast alike.[1]

---

[1]Eaton, however, argues that both 3:21 (translated, retaining MT's pointing, as 'Who knows the spirit of man which goes upwards . . .') and 12:7 hint

One value of Qoheleth's silence on this point is the emphasis it gives to disinterested piety. The attraction of a reward in heaven is not present to compete with that of knowing God on earth; nor does Qoheleth offer the righteous any certainty of preferential treatment here and now (7:15; 8:14; 9:2; despite 2:26).

Yet one cannot properly stop where Qoheleth seems to stop. If God calls for man's response and gives him an awareness of eternity (3:11), it can hardly be with a view to God's discarding all but the memory of him. 'If the LORD had meant to kill us' (it was argued in a very different context), 'he would not have accepted a burnt offering . . . , or shown us all these things . . .'.[1] Job glimpsed this implication of what he had experienced (*cf.* pp.67ff., above); so too, evidently, did certain psalmists;[2] and Jesus found nothing less than resurrection implied in God's commitment to the individual whom he accepts (Mt. 22:31–32).

'The end of the matter' (12:13–14) makes no breakthrough into such a hope, but it does bring into full view what has earlier been glimpsed only fitfully and, for the most part, in deep shadow. Now the fear of God emerges as not merely man's duty (that word has been supplied by the translators) but as his very *raison d'être*;[3] and the judgment of God has, as it must have, the last word.

Qoheleth's summarizer has not failed his author.

---

at continued existence (Eaton, *op. cit.*, pp.87f., 151). MT's pointing of 3:21 nevertheless does not preclude the interrogative sense understood by the ancient versions, as Barton points out (*contra* Gesenius), citing *e.g.* the pointing of Nu. 16:22; Lv. 10:19 (*ICC*, pp.112f.).

[1] Manoah's wife, in Jdg. 13:23.

[2] Pss. 16:8–11; 17:14–15; 49:12–15; 73:23–26.

[3] Strictly the phrase in 12:13b means 'for this is every man' – a concentrated way of saying, 'Every man is destined for, and should be wholly absorbed in, this'. (So A. H. McNeile, *An Introduction to Ecclesiastes*, p.94.)

7

Ecclesiastes –
a sample of opinions

'There is scarcely one aspect of the book,' wrote R. Gordis,[1] 'whether of date, authorship or interpretation, that has not been the subject of wide difference of opinion.' The sample that follows will touch only a few fragments of what has been written.

Date and authorship

Until the time of Luther it was taken for granted that Solomon in his old age was the author of Ecclesiastes, and the date therefore the tenth century BC. But while the author wears at times the mantle of Solomon to explore the ultimate rewards of wealth and wisdom, the only name he uses is '(the) Qoheleth'[2], which gives no clue to his date. His style of Hebrew, however, is unlike that of Solomon elsewhere, or indeed of other Old Testament writers, and approaches in some respects that of the later, Mishnaic, Hebrew of the Christian era; hence the remark of Franz Delitzsch that if Solomon wrote Ecclesiastes there could be no history of the Hebrew language.[3] As a lower limit to the date of writing, fragments of this book found at Qumran, datable by their style of script to c.150 BC, make it unlikely that it could have been composed later than about the mid-3rd century BC. Some time between 350 and 250 BC is a common conjecture.[4]

[1]R. Gordis, *Poets, Prophets and Sages* (Indiana University Press, 1971), p.326.
[2]On this title and name, see p.90, footnote 1.
[3]F. Delitzsch, *Canticles and Ecclesiastes* (T. & T. Clark, 1891), p.190.
[4]The linguistic pattern is complicated by Aramaisms, which could point

Patchwork or unity?

Both the form and the content of Ecclesiastes – the frequent
changes of subject and the seeming conflicts of conviction –
have provoked a long succession of explanations, in which
perhaps four stages call for comment.

1. Early Jewish and Christian writers tended to ease some
of the tensions by reinterpreting or expanding the more
provocative passages. *E.g.*, the Targum (Aramaic paraphrase) attributes the opening cry of 'Vanity' to Solomon's
distress on foreseeing the break-up of his kingdom. It rewrites the 'eat and drink' passages to add a moral dimension
to them; and it interprets 'Be not righteous overmuch' (7:16)
as a warning against being unduly lenient in sentencing a
criminal.[1] The early Fathers, for their part, resorted to
allegory and to reading back New Testament doctrines into
the text, at times, in addition to the more reasonable
emphasis on its role as a preparation for the gospel.

2. Starting with Luther there grew up a tendency to view
the book as a compendium of opinions from various sources,
or as a literary debate. Luther conjectured that it was by
Ben Sirach (2nd century BC): 'a sort of Talmud, compiled
from many books, probably from the library of King Pto-
lemy Euergetes of Egypt.'[2] Some 18th-century writers
imagined a dialogue between two philosophers or between a
master and his pupil, or else a record of opinions voiced in
meetings of a larger group. The weakness of all these speculations was the absence of any reference in the text to a
plurality of speakers or sources (as there is in, *e.g.*, the book
of Job, or the Talmud, or the Socratic Discourses).

3. In the late 19th and early 20th centuries, source-
criticism, already dominant in other Old Testament studies,
suggested that the apparent disorder of the book pointed
to a history of interpolations and/or dislocations. Some

---

either to the post-exilic period in general, when Aramaic was increasingly
competing with Hebrew, or merely to a provincial (northern) place of origin
at any period. M. J. Dahood argues strongly for Phoenician linguistic
influence, and sees the author as a Jew of the late 4th century, resident in
Phoenicia and influenced there by Greek thought (*Biblica* 33, 1952,
pp.191–221; and 39, 1958, pp.302–318). G. L. Archer, however, finds in
these Phoenician traits support for ascribing the book to Solomon, who had
close links with Phoenicia. (Art. 'Ecclesiastes', *Zondervan Pictorial
Encyclopedia of the Bible*, 2 (1975), pp.184 ff.)

[1]See the extracts listed in Plumptre, *Ecclesiastes*, pp.79–86.
[2]Luther's *Table Talk*, cited in Barton, p.21.

pioneering theories of this kind went to extreme lengths. In 1884 G. Bickell (with, as Gordis has remarked, 'enviable omniscience') described in minute detail exactly how the fascicles of a larger work, of which Ecclesiastes formed a part, came adrift and were wrongly re-folded and re-assembled, with linking material inserted by one interpolator and some mollifying orthodoxies by another.[1] Scarcely less elaborate was C. Siegfried's hypothesis (1898) of a pessimistic Qoheleth whose book was worked over by no less than eight interpolators and redactors, including an Epicurean Sadducee, various wisdom teachers and a pious believer in divine justice. Among other energetic dissectors of the book, P. Haupt (1905) not only transposed the order of the verses to the point at which an index became necessary to locate them, but regarded only 124 verses out of 222 as relatively original. Not to be outdone, M. Jastrow would discern at least 120 interpolations.[2]

More soberly, A. H. McNeile[3] argued for only an editor (responsible for the third-person references to Qoheleth and for the postscript in 12:9–10), together with a member of the 'wise men', whose 'frigid didactic style is in strong contrast to the heat and sting of Ḳoheleth's complaints', and a pious Jew who strongly objects to much of what he finds, and therefore inserts corrective remarks at intervals and adds the final postscript (12:13–14). Although this analysis leaves the Preacher seldom uninterrupted (McNeile finds close on thirty interventions of varying lengths in these twelve chapters), it is clearly more economical than Siegfried's, and its reduction of alien material to two kinds – proverbial and pious – has appealed to many subsequent commentators, from Barton (*ICC*, 1908) down to the present day.

4. Recently there has been a growing readiness to attribute the cross-currents of this book largely if not entirely to the author's particular cast of mind. If, to use a military analogy, Qoheleth employs guerrilla rather than set-piece tactics, darting at his objectives from ever-changing angles, or if he is volatile in his responses to the flux of human experience, who is to rule this out of order? It can do justice to the contradictions and oddities of existence

---

[1] Apart from its extravagance, the theory founders on the fact that books were not produced in page form until the Christian era.

[2] M. Jastrow, *A Gentle Cynic* (1919).

[3] *An Introduction to Ecclesiastes*, pp.21ff.

which a tidier approach would be tempted to iron out or to ignore.[1]

Opinions, of course, vary considerably over the extent and nature of this unity-in-diversity. R. Gordis, for example, sees the book as 'a literary unit, the spiritual testament of a single, complex, richly endowed personality', and suggests that it is 'best described as a *cahier* or notebook, into which the author jotted down his reflections during the enforced leisure of old age'.[2] More elaborately, K. Galling analysed the book into 37[3] self-contained pieces written by Qoheleth in various circumstances and moods, and brought together by him without any attempt to play down their differences or heterodoxies. Although Galling rejects sayings on retribution (except 2:26 and 7:26), and alleges some minor glosses, he attributes the bulk of the book, up to 12:8, to the one author.[4]

In a much stronger statement than this, H. W. Hertzberg wrote: 'The more I have occupied myself with Qoh, the more the *unity* [his italics] of Qoh 1:2 – 12:8 has impressed itself on me on all counts . . .'. He quotes with approval R. Windel's remark that as soon as one admits interpolations in a book as episodic as this, the door is wide open to caprice.[5] Hertzberg sees a strong influence of Genesis 1 – 4 on the book, and in line with this he accepts as genuine the sayings about a judgment to come, interpreting them as references to the sentence of death imposed on man at the Fall. (In his view, the epilogue, speaking of judgment on men's *deeds*, introduces a different idea; but O. Loretz, while concurring with Hertzberg's main contention, has pointed out that while Qoheleth does not promise long life as a reward of righteousness, neither does the epilogue.[6])

Even the apparently haphazard structure of Ecclesiastes may conceal a high degree of organization, according to some writers. A. G. Wright[7] has listed a large number of

---

[1]For a discussion of this atomistic and provocative approach, and a comparison of it with the teaching methods of Jesus, see J. G. Williams, *Those Who Ponder Proverbs* (Almond Press, 1981), esp. chapter 3.

[2]*Poets, Prophets and Sages*, p.349.

[3]In a later edition Galling revised this estimate to 34.

[4]*Prediger Salomo*, p.49.   [5]H. W. Hertzberg, *Der Prediger*, p.41 and n.6.

[6]O. Loretz, *Qohelet und der alter Orient*, pp.290–292. Loretz also draws attention to the point made by J. Fichtner (*BZAW* 62 (1933), p.66 n.7) that in the Wisdom books 'judgment' tends to mean the reversals of fortune which God brings in this life.

[7]'The Riddle of the Sphinx', *CBQ* 30 (1968), pp.313–334; reprinted in *SAIW*, pp.245–266.

suggested analyses by various commentators (to which may now be added that of M. A. Eaton[1]), but points out the wide variation between them, and offers what he claims to be a more objective approach through the technique of the 'New Stylistics', or Structural Analysis. Applying this, he isolates the major refrains to mark the main divisions of the book,[2] and suggests in addition a complete series of 'inclusions' and occasional 'dividers' to articulate the smaller paragraphs. For all its close attention to the text, however, this analysis has its own artificialities, since not all of Wright's instances of 'not finding' or 'not knowing' appear to mark stages in the argument. Also, with a writer so fond of using repetitions and catch-phrases it is all too easy to find matching expressions to construe as 'inclusions' or section-markers; and under this rigid scheme the book appears to lose something of its vitality and range. Wright himself points out that if one accepts his findings, Ecclesiastes 'speaks more clearly, but . . . says much less, than we previously thought'.[3]

A more flexible though even more elaborate analysis is proposed by J. A. Loader,[4] who sees the book as consisting of a series of separate pericopes, each of them most carefully structured in one or another of the typical wisdom-literature forms, and each contributing to the general picture, but not so as to provide a logical progress of thought throughout the book. Rather, each one is designed to demonstrate an unresolved tension in some area of life – hence any attempt to relieve these tensions by postulating insertions by glossators and redactors would be misconceived. 'It is part and parcel of Qohelet's polemics to attack "orthodox" utterances by building these into his literary units.'[5] They are quoted in order to be faced with their polar opposites.

This last observation agrees with a certain trend in Qoheleth studies towards accounting for the confessions of faith, or at least for the words of traditional wisdom, not as interpolations nor yet at their face-value, but as targets for Qoheleth's scepticism. His placing of them next to sayings that appear to modify or contradict them acts (on this view)

---

[1]Eaton, *op. cit.*, pp.52f. Eaton's analysis, in outline, is: I. Pessimism: its problems and its remedy (1:1 – 3:22); II. Life 'under the sun' (4:1 – 10:20); III. The call to decision (11:1 – 12:8); IV. Epilogue (12:9–14).

[2]These are 'chasing after wind', in 1:12 – 6:9; and 'not find' and 'not know' in 7:1 – 11:6.

[3]Wright, *art. cit.*, Conclusion.

[4]J. A. Loader, *Polar Structures in the Book of Qohelet*.

[5]*Ibid.*, pp. 132f.

as a tacit criticism. It is a hypothesis that has the great merit of economy. What few scholars trouble to discuss, however, is the possibility that Qoheleth's criticism cuts the other way; *i.e.* that faith in God's justice is, at the very least, 'the Ariadne thread' (in Franz Delitzsch's phrase) 'by which Koheleth at last brings himself safely out of the labyrinth of his scepticism';[1] or better still, that the Preacher's point is (as Eaton has put it) 'that what is to be seen with sheer pessimism "under the sun" may be seen differently in the light of faith in the generosity of God'.[2] As in Ecclesiastes 8:10–12, *'I saw . . .'* has to yield in the end to *'yet I know . . .'*. Both these alternative lines of interpretation are explored in chapter 6, above.

The standpoint of Qoheleth

Some interpretations have been touched on already in discussing the composition of the book. Here we can sample a few in more detail.

Greek influence was keenly debated in the 19th century. From as far back as Zirkel's *Untersuchungen* (1792) a succession of scholars, including Hitzig (1847), Graetz (1871) and Tyler (1874), had drawn up lists of Greek idioms supposedly reflected in the book, and of passages thought to echo Greek ideas. E. H. Plumptre pictured Qoheleth as a kind of prodigal son, swept off his feet by the sensual and intellectual delights of Hellenic Alexandria, before becoming disillusioned and finding his way home to his Creator.[3] C. Cornill, in a famous remark, said that 'Old Testament piety has nowhere enjoyed a greater triumph than in the book of Koheleth'; but he meant the somewhat hollow triumph of a faith that managed to coexist with Greek ideas which were really incompatible with it. Qoheleth was 'in head a Greek, in heart a Jew'.[4] Some analysts of the book into separate sources pressed the matter further by distinguishing between Stoic and Epicurean voices.

The linguistic arguments, however, were answered in detail by Delitzsch and others;[5] while in regard to Greek philosophy G. A. Barton, for one, pointed out the 'striking

[1]F. Delitzsch, *Canticles and Ecclesiastes*, p.441.
[2]Eaton, *op. cit.*, p.45.
[3]*Ecclesiastes*, pp.49ff.
[4]*Introduction to the Canonical Books of the Old Testament* (Eng. edn., 1907), pp.451, 455.
[5]*E.g.*, Delitzsch, pp.190–198; McNeile, pp.39–43; Barton, pp.32f.

contrast' between Qoheleth's position and some of the basic tenets of the Stoics and of the Epicureans, while not wishing to deny the points at which his thoughts ran parallel to those of his Hellenized contemporaries.[1] McNeile, for his part, put it that while Qoheleth shows no influence of any branch of Greek philosophy, yet 'as a thinking Jew he had the makings of a Greek philosopher'.[2] At the same time McNeile drew the contrast between Qoheleth's 'Semitic earnestness' as he 'flings himself against fate', and the Greek ideal of *ataraxia*, imperturbability.[3]

This Semitic and Near Eastern heritage is now increasingly taken into account; moreover Qoheleth is seen as interacting strongly with his own people's traditional wisdom, as in part its debtor and in part its radical critic. G. von Rad expressed this relationship by describing the book as 'a sceptical marginal note on the tradition of the wise men', resting 'wholly upon the traditional themes of the Wisdom literature, though freely glossing them'.[4] This scepticism von Rad saw as the end of a road on which, in his opinion, Israel had already set foot in losing faith in God's action in history. Under this doubt, God's will had now become for Qoheleth something unknowable, therefore the only course left was to accept and enjoy such good things as God happened to give, counting on nothing beyond them.

In this, von Rad chimes in with perhaps a majority of recent writers, if one allows for some different nuances and tones of voice. R. Gordis has written persuasively of Qoheleth as a reluctant cynic, whose love of justice and search for truth were both alike disappointed; who therefore fell back on the one remaining clue to God's will for man, namely the impulse he had implanted towards attaining happiness. In expounding this thesis Qoheleth had to use familiar terms with sometimes an unfamiliar slant (according to Gordis), so that for example in 2:26 a 'sinner' (a word which Gordis puts in inverted commas here) means one who is fool enough not to work for his own happiness. Again, at 11:9, where Qoheleth invites the young man to follow his impulses but reminds him of a day of reckoning, Gordis takes this reference to judgment as intended to be a spur rather than a check, citing a Talmudic saying as a perfect analogy:

Every man must render an account before God, for all the

---

[1]Barton, pp.34–43.   [2]McNeile, p.44.   [3]*Ibid.*, pp.52f.
[4]G. von Rad, *Old Testament Theology*, I, p.455.

good things he beheld in life and did not enjoy.[1]

Whereas Gordis, however, sees grief behind this cheer-fulness, and describes Ecclesiastes as the 'cry of a sensitive spirit, wounded by man's cruelty and folly',[2] H. L. Ginsberg projects Qoheleth's hedonism in more robust, not to say brutal terms. Like Gordis, Ginsberg redefines some stand-ard words, making the expressions 'good in [God's] sight' and 'sinner' (2:26, AV) mean as little as 'lucky' and 'unlucky'. He allows that his author is sensitive to social wrongs and disgusted by shallow merrymaking; but Qoheleth's only idea of any 'plus' in life (*i.e.* any 'profit', 'good' or 'portion') is the enjoyment of one's possessions.[3] So he sums up 2:3–26 as 'I had a large fortune . . . and had the good sense to apply it to the gratification of my desires (3–10). *And that was all I ever did get out of it*'. Morever the 'good sense' which he mentions was the arbitrary gift of God, who gives it only to the fortunate. It seems something of an understatement when he sums up this Qoheleth as 'not altogether orthoprax and certainly by no means orthodox'.[4]

J. G. Williams differs from Ginsberg over bracketing together 'profit' and 'portion' in Qoheleth's thought, for there can be no profit-taking if all is 'vapour and herding of the wind'. But there is a 'portion' which one may be allotted, namely the ability to *enjoy* what one experiences. Apart from that, there is nothing within man's reach. His alien-ation from ultimate reality ('ōlām) is 'unhealable' – for '*per-haps God does not want man to attain this 'ōlām'*, this anti-thesis to 'vanity'.[5] Nor is there any prospect of a divine judgment to set everything right; indeed the concept of 'right' (ṣdq) is no longer a clue to reality.

This widespread opinion, that a moderate hedonism is all that is left to Qoheleth, is not unchallenged. On the one hand the book itself, as it meets us in the canon of Scripture, denies such a verdict and affirms, instead, that the fear of God is the point to which the search has led.[6] Among those

---

[1]Jerusalem Talmud, *Kiddushin*, end; cited in Gordis, *Poets, Prophets and Sages*, p.345.

[2]*Ibid.*, p.350.

[3]Ginsberg regards the verb and noun which are usually translated 'toil' ('āmal, 'āmāl) as having nearly always the sense of earning or acquisition.

[4]H. L. Ginsberg, 'The Structure and Contents of the Book of Koheleth', *VTS* 3 (1955), p.147.

[5]J. G. Williams, 'What does it profit a man?', *Judaism* 20 (1971), p.182 (179–193), reprinted in *SAIW*, p.378 (375–389). The italics are his.

[6]The previous chapter (pp.90ff.) examines the book from this angle.

who accept this positive position we may mention O. Loretz, who is satisfied that this conclusion in the epilogue (12:13–14) rests on authentic sayings in the body of the book.[1] It may be an exaggeration, he concedes, to call Ecclesiastes the 'Song of songs of the fear of God' (Delitzsch, p.183), but that fear is what Qoheleth undoubtedly affirms.[2]

Towards the opposite extreme there are those who would be inclined to darken even the expression 'moderate hedonism'. Crenshaw points out that Qoheleth's 'so-called positive advice' is sprinkled with 'a heavy dose of extract from bitter herbs'. The enjoyment which the Preacher recommends makes existence endurable, but nothing more, on one's 'journey into nothingness'.[3] With an equally pungent metaphor, Loader puts it that in other protest-literature of the ancient Near East the tension is always eventually discharged, the headache followed by relaxation – 'but in Qohelet's head the migraine throbs continually'.[4]

The function of Ecclesiastes in Scripture

Some of the interpretations above carry their own implications for the role of this book in the scheme of revelation, but we may mention a few specific opinions. Some writers, especially those within Judaism, see a rather modest place for it, as encouraging an honest facing of the darkest facts of life, while courageously affirming its delights and refusing to abandon belief in God. Gordis puts this with a flourish, saying of Qoheleth, 'It is his secret wish that men after him . . . may face life with truth as their banner, and with a song in their hearts.'[5] J. G. Williams sees this limited ambition as a less stirring programme than reform, or liberation, or justice, or the vision of God, yet as having something at least in common with the end-time vision of 'every man under his vine and his fig tree'.[6] Much more radically, Crenshaw twice refers to the scepticism of the sages (*i.e.* supremely that of Qoheleth and, in his view, Agur) as providing 'a world view which offered a *viable alternative to the Yahwistic one*'[7] – *i.e.* a view which discounted God's control of history, his spoken

[1]Loretz refers to 3:14; 5:6 (EV 7); 7:18; 8:12–13.
[2]O. Loretz, *Qohelet und der alter Orient*, pp.290f.
[3]J. L. Crenshaw, *Old Testament Wisdom: an Introduction*, pp. 142, 144.
[4]J. A. Loader, *Polar Structures in the Book of Qohelet*, p.123.
[5]Gordis, *Poets, Prophets and Sages*, p.342.
[6]Williams, *art. cit.*, conclusion.
[7]J. L. Crenshaw, *Old Testament Wisdom*, p.190 (his italics); *cf.* p. 238.

revelation and his covenant with Israel; leaving truth to be discovered only through observation and reflection.

Towards the other end of the spectrum can be seen varieties of the view that Qoheleth in one sense or another was preparing the way of the LORD: whether by his onslaught on human *hybris* and (as Loader puts it) on 'fossilized system-theology'[1]; or, more constructively, by his exposure of the hopelessness and untenability of the secularist view of life, thereby indirectly pointing to its alternative (a very different estimate from Crenshaw's, above).[2] More specifically, a number of writers, post-critical as well as pre-critical, have affirmed the traditional Christian view of this book as a preparation for the New Covenant. 'Koheleth,' said Franz Delitzsch, 'from amid his heaps of ruins, shows how necessary it is that the heavens should now soon open above the earth.'[3] H. W. Hertzberg is no less emphatic, concluding that beyond Qoheleth's comprehensive verdict of vanity the only hope for man lay in the 'New Creature' of the New Testament. In this sense, 'The book of Qohelet, standing at the end of the Old Testament, is the most striking messianic prophecy the Old Testament has to offer'.[4] He quotes Vischer's rhetorical question: 'If the Preacher was not right in asserting that all is vanity . . ., that man cannot either obtain or achieve justice, that death is ultimately the only certainty . . . why then did Christ come from God's eternal throne above the sun and die outside Jerusalem for the *redemption* of the whole world?'[5]

Finally, Loretz, in a more cautious appraisal, sees the position not primarily in terms of Qoheleth's negative preparation for the gospel, but rather in the fact that here, as elsewhere in the Old Testament, we listen to the one God who spoke in time past 'in many and various ways' before speaking to us in his Son. We therefore need to hear the divine word here in the form in which it meets us, rather than hastening at once to specify its relation to the New Testament, or to fit Qoheleth into our modern categories of pessimism and the like. In this book man's transience is confronted with God's eternity; but whether God will lead man out of his predicament Qoheleth does not know.

[1] J. A. Loader, *op. cit.*, p.133.
[2] *Cf.* A. Lauha, *Kohelet* (Neukirchner Verlag, 1978), p.191.
[3] F. Delitzsch, *Canticles and Ecclesiastes*, p.184.
[4] H. W. Hertzberg, *Der Prediger*, pp.237f.
[5] W. Vischer, *Zwischen den Zeiten* (München, 1926), p.193, cited in Hertzberg, *op. cit.*, p.238, n.27.

This candour (Loretz points out) brought Qoheleth the reputation of one whose faith was in jeopardy: a cheerless pessimist and sceptic. *But the New Testament upholds the verdict of 'vanity'*, while deepening our understanding of it by showing that the creation was subjected to it 'in hope; because the creation itself will be set free from its bondage to decay and obtain the glorious liberty of the children of God' (Rom. 8:20–21).

Thus Qoheleth holds up the mirror to man, showing him the transience of his work and the fact that God's work alone endures. This is the corrective which man needs to his perennial conviction that he can make unlimited progress; for until the end of the age and the break-in of God's full reign, Paul's words in Romans 8:20ff. still apply to us. But whereas Qoheleth can only say that God's work alone will last, Paul proclaims that God has acted in Christ, and that the groaning and travail of the present age will not be in vain.[1]

[1]O. Loretz, *op. cit.*, pp.307–315.

8

Voices in counterpoint
The three books compared,
contrasted and integrated

If one had to design a cover for each of the three canonical wisdom books, drawn from their own contents, one might represent them by the various houses they describe. For Proverbs it could appropriately be the seven-pillared house of Wisdom, or better still that gracious, well-stocked home of the accomplished wife, whose virtues bring the book to its serene close. For Job, a very different picture: perhaps the wreckage in which his family perished when 'a great wind came across the wilderness, and struck the four corners of the house'; or perhaps even the ash heap to which he banished himself. As for Ecclesiastes, its insistence on the transience of earthly glory could hardly find a better symbol than its own description of a great house (12:3–4) in the grip of slow, inexorable decay.

Between them, the three books clearly cover three aspects of existence which no-one can afford to overlook: the demands of practical good management; the enigma of calamities that are beyond control or explanation; and the tantalizing hollowness and brevity of human life.

But what of the interplay between the three? – for they will hardly have been written in total ignorance of one another or of the different emphases within the wisdom tradition which has nurtured them all.

Some writers would argue that while Job reacts against the optimism of Proverbs, Ecclesiastes reacts against them both, questioning even the hidden benevolence of God which Job accepted in the end.[1] But a more common view is that

---

[1]For such a view of Ecclesiastes (also of Agur, given an emended and circumscribed text), see above, pp.52f., 112f.

both Job and Ecclesiastes are reacting in their different ways against the traditional wisdom embodied in Proverbs. Archbishop Blanch has put this view outspokenly in a popular survey of the Old Testament:

> The tone [of Proverbs] is sententious or, if you prefer a shorter word, smug, and it suffers from one grave defect which has been the death of many such a philosophy ever since. It suggests that the study and practice of Wisdom will issue in peace, happiness and success. It could not be better put than at the end of chapter 11 in the book of Proverbs: 'The righteous shall be recompensed in the earth'. The book of Ecclesiastes ... undermined that belief with a kind of sapping action; the book of Job assaults it with all the artillery at the author's command.[1]

The truth, however, is more complex than this, and the relation of Proverbs to both of its neighbours needs a closer look.

Proverbs and Job

There is no denying that Job's comforters (whose views the book repudiates) rely on the kind of generalizations that abound in Proverbs. Who could be sure, for instance, which of the two books produces which of the following remarks?

> Surely vexation kills the fool,
>> and jealousy slays the simple.
>
> No ill befalls the righteous,
>> but the wicked are filled with trouble.
>
> The light of the righteous rejoices,
>> but the lamp of the wicked will be put out.
>
> Yea, the light of the wicked is put out,
>> and the flame of his fire does not shine.[2]

But the use that the two make of these sentiments is not the same. While Proverbs treats them as a spur to faith and faithfulness, the comforters of Job make them a rod for his back. The spirit of the former is, 'How reassuring for us!', but of the latter, 'How damning for you!' – while Job for his part dares to ask,

---

[1] S. Y. Blanch, *For All Mankind* (Bible Reading Fellowship, [2]1977), p.11.
[2] Jb. 5:2; Pr. 12:21; 13:9; Jb. 18:5.

> How often *is* it that the lamp of the wicked is put out?
>
> Jb. 21:17.

Job's question is one that Proverbs scarcely raises, yet scarcely disallows. For all its optimism, Proverbs is not blind to the anomalies of life: it is aware of innocent people who meet a violent end (1:11; 6:17) or are cheated of their rights (17:23,26; 18:5) or of their livelihood (13:23). What it does not envisage, however, is any possibility that *God* may act unjustly (the thought that haunted Job); but on this again there is something more to be said.

First, it is at least possible that Proverbs, like Job himself, is impelled at times by the logic of its own faith to look beyond the horizon of death to see the righteous and the wicked recompensed. True, some injustices will be redressed simply through the verdict of history –

> The memory of the righteous is a blessing,
> but the name of the wicked will rot
>
> Pr. 10:7.

– or through the later fortunes of one's family:

> The wicked are overthrown and are no more,
> but the house of the righteous will stand.
>
> Pr. 12:7.

But a few sayings seem to press the matter further. One such is 14:32, according to the Hebrew text (preserved in RSV margin; *cf.* AV, RV, NIV):

> The wicked is overthrown through his evil-doing,
> but the righteous finds refuge in his death.[1]

'To take refuge' implies almost invariably refuge in the LORD, in the Old Testament; hence BDB's rendering: '*A righteous man in his death seeketh refuge* (in Yahweh).' If the Hebrew text is right, the contrast between the first and second lines makes death the great divide instead of the great leveller – a vision akin to that of Psalm 49:14–15, or Psalm 73. It also suggests a more than temporal dimension to the saying in Proverbs 11:7,

> When the wicked dies, his hope perishes,
> and the expectation of the godless comes to naught

---

[1] The alternative to 'in his death' (*bᵉmôtô*) arises from transposing the Heb. consonants to read, with LXX, Syr, *bᵉtummô*, 'in his integrity', as most modern versions prefer to do. This, however, looks suspiciously like the avoidance of a bold saying.

– though this cannot be pressed. It may look no further than the abrupt end of all his plans. For the righteous, however, there is one tantalizingly cryptic saying which may have the defeat of death in view: for while most modern versions emend the text of Proverbs 12:28, to read the opposite of its apparent meaning, both BDB and Dahood find immortality affirmed in it.[1] So NIV agrees substantially with AV, RV, in rendering this verse:

> In the way of righteousness there is life;
> along that path is immortality.

Secondly, although it is at best an open question whether or not these passages catch a glimpse of requital beyond death, the completed Scripture has no doubt of it. Proverbs turns out to have spoken more wisely than it could have known; less 'smugly' than it might appear. The meek *will* inherit the earth, we are now assured, and both evil and evildoers will be rooted out.[2] So we can improve on the statement that this book deals in generalities. It does so indeed (for well-doing does generally tend towards well-being, however large a minority the exceptions may constitute), but it also deals in ultimates – for we find that we can say Amen to its strong certainties after all, in the light of what has subsequently been revealed.

Meanwhile, those who had to wrestle with injustice without this light found the certainties of Proverbs and its companions either a temptation to apply them with blind dogmatism (as did Job's comforters), or else such a sharpening of the problem as to drive them first towards despair and then towards Job's own breakthrough into resurrection-hope. That hope had become common property, to all but Sadducees,[3] by the end of the Old Testament era.

Proverbs and Ecclesiastes

The relation between Proverbs and Ecclesiastes illustrates what in modern jargon might be called 'creative conflict', or more simply the principle that 'iron sharpens iron' (as Pr. 27:17 puts it) – for Qoheleth makes some of his sharpest

---

[1] *'And the journey of her pathway is no-death!'*, BDB, p.677a, *s.v. nāṯîb. Cf. ibid.*, p.39a, *s.v. 'al*, b., c. See also M. J. Dahood, *Biblica* 41 (1960), pp.176–181; and his *Proverbs and Northwest Semitic Philology* (Rome, 1963), p.28. For a criticism of Dahood see McKane, *ad loc.*

[2] *Cf., e.g.*, Mt. 5:5; 13:41.   [3] *Cf.* Jn. 11:24; Mt. 22:23; Acts 23:6ff.

observations in apparent reaction to the clear-cut axioms of Proverbs. He does not have to quote the book, but its well-known sayings on the rewards of hard work, the blessings of wisdom and the short-lived gains of wickedness (to name a few of its themes) give a specially hard edge to his contrary remarks.

Yet, in each case, Qoheleth's overall response to this traditional wisdom is not a total denial but a virtual *'Yes – but . . .'.*[1] This can be illustrated in relation to the three themes we have mentioned.

a. On work and wealth, we have his *'Yes'* in, *e.g.*, Ecclesiastes 10:18–19:

> Through sloth the roof sinks in,
> and through indolence the house leaks.
> Bread is made for laughter,
> and wine gladdens life,
> and money answers everything.

'But' that is not the whole story. So we have the salutary reminder that not only money (5:10) but work itself can become, in our terms, an addiction – so that its victim never stops, and 'never asks, "For whom am I toiling . . .?"' (4:7–8). Again, its precious rewards may all be lost in one 'bad venture', and certainly will elude us in the end (5:13–17). Or a man may make a fortune and lose the power to enjoy it (6:1–6) – or find it eaten up by human parasites (5:11). Absurdly, he may simply have too much of everything to let him sleep (5:12), whether we are to take it as too much worry on his mind, or time on his hands, or just food on his stomach.

b. Then on wisdom and its blessings: certainly Qoheleth values this quality as Proverbs does, both for itself and for its benefits.

> Wisdom excels folly as light excels darkness.
>
> 2:13.
>
> Wisdom gives strength to the wise man . . .
>
> 7:19.
>
> A man's wisdom makes his face shine . . .
>
> 8:1.

---

[1]*Cf.* J. C. Rylaarsdam, *Proverbs to Song of Solomon* (SCM Press, 1964), p.110.

'*But*' other things need saying. In this ungrateful world, wisdom may get scant regard. In the story of the poor man who 'by his wisdom delivered the city, ... no one remembered that poor man' (9:13–16). And how vulnerable it is! It takes only 'one sinner' to destroy its patient work; only 'a little folly' to discredit it (9:18; 10:1). More seriously, the wisest man can only scratch the surface of reality:

> I said, 'I will be wise'; but it was far from me. That which is, is far off, and deep, very deep; who can find it out? (7:23–24).

Finally, it has no answer to death or to the obliterating hand of time.

> For ... in the days to come all will have been long forgotten. How the wise man dies just like the fool! (2:16).

c. As for the end in store for the wicked, once again Qoheleth gives his '*Yes*' to the conviction of traditional wisdom:

> Though a sinner does evil a hundred times and prolongs his life, yet I know that it will be well with those who fear God ...; but it will not be well with the wicked ... (8:12–13).

Yet in the short run there is an emphatic '*But*' to be immediately considered. For Qoheleth continues:

> There is a vanity which takes place on earth, that there are righteous men to whom it happens according to the deeds of the wicked, and there are wicked men to whom it happens according to the deeds of the righteous. I said that this also is vanity (8:14; *cf.* 7:15).

More scandalously still, men are so dazzled by success that the really brazen sinner is quite likely to be lionized – almost canonized –

> Then I saw the wicked buried; they used to go in and out of the holy place, and were praised[1] in the city where they had done such things. This also is vanity (8:10).

Faced with such human caprice, added to that of 'time and

---

[1]So most modern versions, following LXX and some Heb. MSS. Even MT's 'forgotten' would suggest, in this context of laxity at 'the holy place', a short memory for their misdeeds, rather than repudiation of their names.

chance', which ignores our merits and demerits,[1] Qoheleth at one point lets moral cynicism have its say:

> Be not righteous overmuch, and do not make yourself overwise; why should you destroy yourself? Be not wicked overmuch, neither be a fool; why should you die before your time? (7:16–17).

Whether this is a momentary reaction in a dark hour, or (as I would hold) his exposure of the secularist's implicit, unheroic motto, it is an outlook that cannot ultimately live with the conviction, expressed at intervals elsewhere, of a coming judgment.[2] Qoheleth's godly '*Yes*' on this point, whatever contradictions the present vanity may suggest, must be given eventually the last word – which means that his book will end, through the inspired insight of his editor, where Proverbs had begun: with the fear of the LORD God who weighs up every deed and motive. The Alpha of Proverbs has become the Omega of Ecclesiastes.

At a less overtly theological level, that of style and manner, Proverbs and Ecclesiastes display at times their common background of aphoristic wisdom. Some of Qoheleth's sentence-sayings are indistinguishable from those of Proverbs – at least at first sight. But are they in fact subtly different, reassuring us only to spring a surprise?

Certainly some have a powerful sting in the tail, as we noticed in an earlier chapter (p.101). Take for instance Ecclesiastes 7:1,

> A good name is better than precious ointment,

with its devastating sequel,

> and the day of death, than the day of birth.

A provocative opening can be equally disturbing:

> Sorrow is better than laughter . . .

7:3.

– or a comfortable proverb, complete in itself, may be given a companion which shatters it. For example:

> He who is joined to all the living has hope, for a living dog is better than a dead lion

---

[1] 'Again I saw that under the sun the race is not to the swift . . .' (9:11), *etc.*
[2] See again 8:12–13; also 3:17; 11:9; and, in the epilogue, 12:13–14.

– to which the next verse mercilessly adds:

> For the living know that they will die, but the dead know nothing . . . (9:4–5).

Elsewhere, too, a comparable shadow falls across Qoheleth's praise of simple joys, with the reminder that these things too are vanity:

> . . . for there is no work or thought or knowledge or wisdom in Sheol, to which you are going.[1]

This technique, this lurking *'But . . .'* waiting to unsettle our most secure assumptions, may explain the presence of a number of conventional sayings which an earlier generation of critics ascribed to orthodox interpolators. This, we can now see, is still Qoheleth speaking, but ready to pounce. Often, though, he cites or creates an uncontroversial proverb 'simply because he agrees with it' (as Gordis sensibly remarks[2]) – for there are many straight sayings which have no trip-wire concealed within or next to them. Besides, this restless and candid thinker is the last person we should accuse of being the mere prisoner of his own scepticism, duty-bound to discredit whatever faith or common sense might say. For all his questionings, he has no quarrel with conservative wisdom, as long as it is not the means of hiding from us the darker facts of life which it is his mission to expose.

Uncomfortable companion though he is, Qoheleth is the ally, not the enemy, of his fellow observers of the human scene.

Conclusion

At the start of this chapter we used the analogy of the three houses – prosperous, stricken and decaying – to highlight the diversity of the three books and their consequent coverage of an extensive area of life. It is worth pointing out that this single-minded pursuit of their respective interests is typical of the Old Testament's way of doing things. It tends to give itself wholly to one thing at a time, saying it with maximum force and leaving any resulting imbalance to be corrected in due course by an equally massive counter-

---

[1]Ec. 9:10. *Cf.*, in relation to their cheerful contexts, the momentary chill in 2:26c; 3:22; 5:20; 8:15; 11:8,10.

[2]R. Gordis, *Poets, Prophets and Sages*, p.346.

weight. In this way more justice can be done to a many-sided subject than by steering a middle course between its extremes. It also makes for colour and vitality, in contrast to the convoluted style in which every statement must be qualified as soon as made.

To pick up the title of this chapter, our three books in synthesis can be compared to voices in vigorous counter-point – heard together, yet each contributing its distinctive statement to the whole. Job, to be sure, is a piece of counter-point in itself, with its clash of separate voices; so too is Ecclesiastes with Qoheleth's inward dialogue. And Pro-verbs? This again has many voices, but chiefly in straight-forward concord rather than in mutual confrontation. As the two sections of this chapter have suggested, Proverbs (or the standard wisdom which it represents) tends to make the statements which give the other books their impulse to join in. It is like the *canto fermo* (the measured tread of a familiar tune) round which the other voices, other choirs even, weave their patterns and produce their concords and calculated dissonances.

Some of these dissonances, as we have seen, are readily resolved; others urge us forward to the New Testament; others again are still with us, putting into words the 'groaning in travail' which the New Testament itself accepts as irreducible in the present age. But 'travail' is an expec-tant word.

Wisdom, then, by this tension between its three main expositions, presents itself not only as located in God, foun-ded (for mankind) in reverence and expressed in obedience,[1] but orientated towards the ending of this present 'vanity' to which the creation is 'subjected . . . in hope'.[2]

Only at that consummation shall we 'understand fully, even as (we) have been fully understood'.[3] But I doubt if at that point we shall still call it wisdom.

---

[1]Pr. 3:19; Jb. 28:28; Pr. 1:7; Ec. 12:13.   [2]Rom. 8:18–25.
[3]1 Cor. 13:12.

Appendix A

Some international reflections on life

In the opening chapter we noticed Israel's awareness of wise men beyond her borders; and we have mentioned some of their writings and sayings in the chapters on Proverbs, Job and Ecclesiastes. The following extracts show a little of the kind of thinking that was current in some circles abroad, about the areas of life which these three biblical books explored. Much of it was copied and re-copied during the second millennium BC and onward, from the time 'when Israel was a child' to the days of her kings, prophets and psalmists. Throughout her history, this was part of the intellectual climate of the world with which she traded, fought and fraternized.

The three sections of this chapter correspond broadly with the three canonical wisdom books: Proverbs, Job and Ecclesiastes, in that order.

Instructions and precepts

Most of the extracts here are from the writings of administrators for the benefit of their sons or successors, advising them on the qualities which make for professional stability and success. Many of these texts were subsequently used as teaching material for students to copy out. Those that are quoted here range over a period of some 2,000 years, from Ptah-Hotep (c.2450 BC) to Onchsheshonqy (4th century BC?), and geographically from Egypt to Mesopotamia. They are well worth reading in full, and most of them are reasonably accessible.[1]

[1]The widest range is in *ANET* and its 1969 Supplement (or its 3rd

Because a writer would often drive home a point with some pithy saying, which might be either proverbial or original – and there is usually no way of knowing which – there is no attempt here to separate popular from literary aphorisms. Nor is this selection meant to summarize a culture or a period. The available material naturally ranges from occasional heights to occasional depths, but with plenty of everyday good sense in between. Here we shall sample only a fraction of the teachings and sayings which have some common ground with the interests of the book of Proverbs.

Justice and integrity

As in the biblical Proverbs, what is right is seen as what is eminently wise, whatever the immediate attractions of the easier way.

> Wrongdoing has never brought its undertaking into port. (It may be that) it is fraud that gains riches, (but) the strength of justice is that it lasts, and a man may say: "It is the property of my father." Ptah-Hotep (Egypt, *c*.2450 BC). (*ANET*, p.412b).

> If riches are brought to thee by robbery,
> They will not spend the night with thee . . .
> They have made themselves wings like geese
> And are flown away to the heavens.
> Amenemope (Egypt, late 2nd millennium BC?), ch.16
> (*ANET*, p.423b). (*Cf.* Pr. 10:2; 23:4–5; 28:20.)

A ruler should be as fair at home as he is in court:

At home:

> Speak justice in thy (own) house . . . It is the forepart of the house [the master's part] that inspires respect in the back [the servants' quarters]. (*Cf.* Jb. 31:13–15; Pr. 11:29.)

In court:

> Do justice whilst thou endurest upon earth. Quiet the

edition), under the heading 'Didactic and Wisdom Literature'. For fuller Mesopotamian material see *BWL* and E. I. Gordon's *Sumerian Proverbs*. For Ahikar see R. H. Charles, *Apocrypha and Pseudepigrapha of the Old Testament*, vol.2, pp.728ff. On Onchsheshonqy there is a useful discussion by B. Gemser in *VTS* 7 (1960), pp.102–128. There is also an extended survey of this literature in McKane's *Proverbs*, pp.51–208.

weeper, do not oppress the widow ... Be on thy guard against punishing wrongfully ... (*Cf.* Pr. 31:8–9.)

In general:

Be not evil: patience is good. Make thy memorial to last through the love of thee ... (*Cf.* Pr. 29:4.)
For King Merikare (Egypt, *c.*2100 BC?) (*ANET*, p.415)

Piety

The chief emphasis falls on cultic acts and their rewards, sometimes in rather calculating terms. King Merikare was advised:

Make monuments ... for the god. This is what preserves the name of him who does it. ... The god is aware of him who works for him. (*ANET*, p.416a)

But while this is the prevailing tone, there is more to it, for the same king was reminded that the god cares more for a good man's character than for a bad man's sacrificial ox (*ANET*, p.417b); *cf.* Pr. 15:8. Likewise in Babylonia, while the Counsels of Wisdom quote the maxims,

Reverence begets favour,
Sacrifice improves life,
And prayer dispels guilt,[1]

they have earlier stressed the pleasure that one's god takes in a man's magnanimity and kindness, adding the precept,

Do good things, be kind all your days.
(*ANET*[3], p.595a)

Generosity

To the poor (*cf.* Pr. 22:9; 29:7; Jb. 31:16ff.):

If thou findest a large debt against a poor man,
Make it into three parts,
Forgive two, and let one stand.
... Thou wilt lie down and sleep (soundly) ...
Amenemope, ch.13 (*ANET*, p.423b)

Eat not ... if another is suffering want, and thou dost not stretch out the hand to him with bread.
Ani (Egypt, late 2nd millennium BC) (Erman, p.239)

[1]*ANET*[3], pp.595–596.

To a personal enemy (*cf.* Pr. 24:17, 29; 25:21):

> . . . we shall not act like him –
> Lift him up, give him thy hand;
> Leave him (in) the arms of the god;
> Fill his belly with bread of thine,
> So that he may be sated and may be ashamed . . .
>
> Amenemope, ch.2 (*ANET*, p.422a)

Likewise, from Mesopotamia:

> Requite with kindness your evildoer,
> Maintain justice to your enemy,
> Smile on your adversary.
> If your ill-wisher is [. . . ,] nurture him.
>
> Counsels of Wisdom (*BWL*, p.101; *cf. ANET*^{3}, p.595a)

Domestic virtues

The advice tends to be worldly-wise, viewing disharmony at home chiefly as a threat to one's career. But it has its moments of sensitivity and warmth, and the two approaches may be unblushingly intermingled.

> If thou art a man of standing, thou shouldst found thy household and love thy wife as it is fitting. Fill her belly; clothe her back. [Provide] ointment for her body. Make her heart glad as long as thou livest. She is a profitable field for her lord. Thou shouldst not contend with her at law; and keep her far from gaining control . . . Her eye is her stormwind . . .
>
> Ptah-Hotep (*ANET*, p.413b)

Here is sensitivity:

> Thou shouldst not supervise (too closely) thy wife when thou knowest that she is efficient. Do not say to her: 'Where is it? Fetch (it) for us!' when she has put (it) in the (most) useful place . . . Recognize her abilities. How happy it is when thy hand is with her! Many . . . do not know what a man should do to stop dissension in his house . . .
>
> Ani (*ANET*, p.421a)

Philandering is seen (as in Proverbs) as both a disaster and a disgrace. Ptah-Hotep, ever professional, observes that by sexual indiscretion,

> a thousand men [may be distracted from] their (own) advantage

– but he also finds it abhorrent in itself:

> Do not do it – it is really an abomination . . .
>
> > *(ANET*, p.413b)

As for the 'woman from abroad, . . . far away from her husband', the Instruction of Ani is as wary of her as are the discourses of Proverbs. She is 'a deep water, whose windings one knows not', and her activities are 'a great crime, (worthy) of death'.[1] The Babylonian Counsels of Wisdom take a look at the slender hope of a stable marriage with an unstable partner:

> Do not marry a prostitute, whose husbands are legion, . . .
> When you have trouble, she will not support you,
> When you have a dispute she will be a mocker.
> There is no reverence or submissiveness in her. . . .
> . . . She pricks up her ears for the footsteps of another man
>
> > *(ANET*[3], p.595b)

Sobriety

The home-truths in Proverbs 23:29–35 about the joys of drink have a less brilliant but equally outspoken counterpart in the Instruction of Ani:

> Boast not (?) that you can drink a jug of beer. You speak, and an unintelligible utterance issues from your mouth. If you fall down and your limbs break, there is no one to hold out a hand to you. Your companions in drink stand up and say: *"Away with this sot!"* If there comes one . . . to question you, you are found lying on the ground, and you are like a little child.[2]

More generally, a teacher's advice:

> Set not your heart after miserable pleasures; they are not profitable, nor do they serve a man against a day of distress.
>
> > Pap. Sallier, I (Caminos, p.312).

Friends

As in Proverbs, friends may get you into trouble (Pr.

---

[1]Instruction of Ani, *ANET*, p.420a. *Cf.* Pr. 2:16–19; 5:3–14; 6:24ff.; 7:10ff.; Ec. 7:26.

[2]Erman, pp.236–237, slightly adapted ('you', *etc.*, replacing 'thou', *etc.*).

22:24–25) or out of trouble (Pr.27:10); and the meeting of minds which is touched on in some of the sayings in Proverbs 27 is persuasively encouraged in the last paragraph below.

> Do not associate with the heated man,
> Nor visit him for conversation.
>> Amenemope, ch.9 (*ANET*, p.423a)

> The companion of a fool is a fool;
> The companion of a wise man is a wise man.
>> Onchsheshonqy 12:6 (McKane, p.126)

> Do not go to your brother if you are in trouble:
> go to your friend.
>> Onchsheshonqy 16:4 (Gemser, *VTS* 7, p.121)

> When you are humiliated, let your friend act.
>> Assyrian Collection 2:33f. (*BWL*, p.232)

> If thou art seeking out the nature of a friend, . . . deal with him alone. . . . Test his heart with a bit of talk. . . . If . . . he should do something with which thou art displeased, behold, he is still a friend. . . . do not trample him down.
>> Ptah-Hotep (*ANET*, p.414a)

The use of words

Be a good listener

> When hearing is good, speaking is good.
>> Ptah-Hotep (*ANET*, p.414a); *cf.* Pr. 18:2,13.

> Be not arrogant because of thy knowledge. . . . Take counsel with the ignorant as well as the wise, for the limits of art cannot be reached, and no artist fully possesseth his skill. A good discourse is more hidden than the precious green stone, and yet it is found with slave girls over the mill stones.
> Ptah-Hotep (Erman, p.56; *cf. ANET*, p.412b); *cf.* Pr. 28:11.

Be cautious

> Thou shouldst not express thy (whole) heart to the stranger, to let him discover thy speech against thee. . . . A man may fall to ruin because of his tongue.
>> Ani (*ANET*, p.420b); *cf.* Pr. 13:3.

Be genuine

Do not cut off thy heart from thy tongue.
>> Amenemope, ch.10 (*ANET*, p.423b);
>> *cf.* Pr. 26:24ff.; 27:5–6.

Be kind

Do not say evil things, speak well of people.
>> Counsels of Wisdom (*BWL*, p.105; *ANET*³, p.595b);
>> *cf.* Pr. 10:11–12; 11:12; 12:18.

Be skilful

Be a craftsman in speech, so that thou mayest prevail,
for the power of (a man) is the tongue, and speech is
mightier than any fighting.
>> Merikare (Erman, pp.73f.; *cf. ANET*, p.415a);
>> *cf.* Pr 15:23; 25:15.

A boy's upbringing

(*cf.* Pr. 4:1 ff.; 13:24; 19:18; 22:6,15; 23:13–14; 29:17):

How good it is when a son accepts what his father says!
Thereby maturity comes to him. He whom god loves is a
hearkener, (but) he whom god hates cannot hear.
>> Ptah–Hotep (*ANET*, p.414a)

Strong words from schoolmasters:

Spend no day in idleness or thou wilt be beaten. The ear
of a boy is on his back, and he hearkens when he is
beaten.
>> Pap. Anastasi 3:13 (Erman, p.189)

Young fellow, how conceited you are! ... Your heart is
heavier than a great monument of a hundred cubits in
height ...
>> Pap. Lansing 19f. (Caminos, p.377)

The ape understands words. ... Lions are trained and
horses tamed: but as for you ...
>> Pap. Bologna 1094 (Caminos, p.13)

Advice to parents:

My son, withhold not thy son from stripes: for the beat-
ing of a boy is like manure to a garden, and like rope to
an ass.
>> Ahikar 2:22 (Charles, p.732)

131

> My son, teach hunger and thirst to thy son, that according
> as his eye sees he may govern his house.
>
> > Ahikar 2:47 (Charles, p.735)

But an Egyptian sage says everything in a sentence:

> Teach him to be a man.
>
> > Ani (*ANET*, p.420a)

Studies of suffering

Of the texts on this theme that have come down to us, those
from Mesopotamia happen to be nearest to the concerns of
Job – although there is superficially a somewhat Job-like
quality in the Egyptian 'Protests of the Eloquent Peasant'
(*c.* 2000 BC),[1] whose complaints of injustice grew more outspoken and more spirited the more he was belaboured for
them. But there the injustice was human, not (as it seemed
to Job) divine, and was prolonged purely for the Pharaoh's
enjoyment of such eloquence. By contrast, the three texts
summarized below are concerned with the attitudes of
heaven to what seem to be the random blows of fate.

Man and his God

This 'Sumerian Variation on the "Job" Motif',[2] from *c.*2000
BC, is a poem of 140 lines, exhorting the reader to 'soothe the
heart of his god' by constant praise and penitence, since 'a
man without a god would not obtain food'.

First it tells how a young man of good character was
suddenly struck down by illness, ruin and ostracism. Then
the man himself pours out his complaint to his god who has
'doled out ... suffering' to him and left him to the tender
mercies of men and demons.

> My companion says not a true word to me,
> My friend gives the lie to my righteous word.
> The man of deceit has *conspired* against me,
> (And) you, my god, do not thwart him.

> On the day shares were allotted to all,
> > my allotted share was suffering.

---

[1] *ANET*, pp.407–410.
[2] Translated by S. N. Kramer, *ANET*[3], pp.589–591; previously published
by him in *VTS* 3 (1960), pp.170–182.

But eventually he calls to mind the saying that all men are sinners:

> Never has a sinless child been born . . .

and he proceeds to seek pardon for whatever wrong he may have done,

> Now that you have shown me my sins.

Then the god is mollified, drives off the tormenting demons, and receives the constant praises of his grateful worshipper.

The poem, in fact, for all its initial likeness to the story of Job, disposes of the problem of unmerited suffering by virtually denying it. If all are sinners, all deserve ill of their god, and need to have this fact brought home to them so that they may soothe his heart by self-abasement and by paying him due honour.

By this answer in terms of guilt and desert, however, the question of *comparative* desert – why the most assiduous worshipper may be the most afflicted – is, if anything, made harder rather than easier to live with.

Ludlul Bēl Nēmeqi
('I will praise the Lord of wisdom')

W. G. Lambert suggests the Cassite period (*c.*1500–1200 BC) for this composition,[1] which has often been known as 'The Babylonian Job'. This title, however, as Lambert points out,[2] seemed appropriate enough when only Tablet II was available, but less so in the light of the fuller text, which emphasizes not so much the mystery of suffering as the sovereignty of Marduk, who both smites and heals.

Tablet I. After much praise of Marduk the lord of wisdom, the speaker (a man who has held high office) comes to his sad story. His personal god and goddess and his guardian spirit have deserted him, leaving him stricken, humiliated, evicted, a social pariah. Like Job (Jb. 7:13–14),

> When I lie down at night, my dream is terrifying,

and like Hezekiah (Is. 38:14),

> I moan like a dove all day long.

---

[1]Translated in *ANET*, pp.434–437 (R. H. Pfeiffer); *BWL*, pp.36–62 (W. G. Lambert); *ANET*³, pp.596–601 (R. D. Biggs).
[2]*BWL*, p.27.

All the omens are bad, and he is dangerous to know:

> For the . . . who says, 'God bless you', death comes at the gallop.[1]

Tablet II. He has survived to the next year, but only just. His prayers are unheard, his diviner gets no message – yet he had been diligent and fervent in religion, and had used his authority to foster reverence for the gods and respect for the king. Had he been mistaken? He now voices a fearful doubt (II.33):

> I wish I knew that these things would be pleasing to one's god

– for perhaps even right and wrong, to us, are their opposites to the gods:

> What in one's own heart seems despicable may be proper to one's god (II.35).

These disturbing reflections are followed by a catalogue of bodily afflictions (viewed as demonic visitants) of every imaginable kind – enough to be the envy of any hospital raconteur ('In my epigastrium they kindled a fire . . .'), bringing him to death's very door.

Suddenly, in the last two lines of this tablet, he dares to say, *'I know . . .'*, in an affirmation which almost seems to anticipate Job's 'Redeemer' saying:

> But I know the day for my whole family,
> When, among my friends, their Sun-god will have mercy.
> > II.119f.

(Yet the likeness brings out at the same time the contrast, since here the sufferer's hope is confined to his family's rehabilitation. There is nothing of Job's intensely personal conviction: 'I shall see God, whom I shall see for myself, and my eyes shall behold, and not another' (Jb. 19:26–27).)

Tablet III. After a few lines of further lament ('His hand was heavy upon me . . .'), the outlook slowly brightens with a series of dreams, in which three glorious beings successively bring the sufferer tokens of divine favour and cleansing, and finally a decree of prosperity from Marduk.

> My illness was quickly over . . . ,
> After the mind of my Lord had quietened

[1]*BWL*, p.35 (I.96).

And the heart of merciful Marduk rejoiced[1]. . .

> III.49–51.

The sickness-demons are banished, each bodily part is set right (even 'my fingernails'!), and the sufferer praises Marduk for his recovery.

Tablet IV rounds off the poem with a psalm of personal thanksgiving.[2]

Two special points of contrast with the book of Job may be noted (in addition to the pervasive polytheism, omens and magical rites). First, the paralysing doubt whether man can know anything at all of heaven's moral values (II.33ff.). Secondly, the fact that the sufferer's afflictions turn out to have been the penalty of a religious lapse. He was not innocent after all. This emerges from his dream of a purifying ritual in Tablet III.21–28, from the allusions to the removal of 'my guilt', *etc.*, at the fragmentary end of that tablet,[3] and finally from the hero's parting advice to the reader (implying that his offence had been a ritual one):

> He who has done wrong in respect to Esagil [the temple of Marduk], let him learn from me!

The problem of unmerited suffering has received, by implication, a similar answer to that of the Sumerian poem, 'Man and his God', above.

The Babylonian Theodicy

On the sentence-acrostic running through the 27 stanzas of this poem, see above, p.55. Although there are only two speakers, their dialogue broadly resembles that of the book of Job by its alternation of bitter protest and would-be orthodox reply. Here, however, the sufferer's friend, unlike Job's comforters, keeps his temper throughout.

Lambert suggests a date in the region of 1000 BC, but finds 'no strong reason to compel any date in particular between about 1400 and 800' (*BWL*, pp.63,67).

Here, taking many liberties, I have attempted to show the progress of the dialogue by summarizing the drift of each

---

[1]Or, 'was appeased' (*BWL*). Fragments of lines 57–59 which are not included in *ANET*[3] (but see *BWL*, p.51; *cf. ANET*[2], p.436b) speak of 'my guilt', 'my iniquity', 'my transgression', followed by 'He made the wind bear away my offences' (III.60).

[2]But Lambert queries the connection of this tablet with the poem (*BWL*, pp.24ff.).

[3]See footnote 1, above.

11-line stanza in a sentence or two.

1. Sufferer: Wisest of men – I'm at my wits' end, and I've no parents – nobody! – to turn to.

2. Friend: You are looking at the dark side! Look to your god and goddess – they will see you through.

3. Sufferer: But listen to the facts. I'm ill, half starved, and there's not a gleam of hope.

4. Friend: These are wild thoughts! Pray, and do what is right, and heaven will smile on you.

5. Sufferer: But answer me this: how pious was that well-fed lion – or that profiteer?

6. Friend: Those predators won't last long! The thing that does last is the blessing of your God.

7. Sufferer: How right that sounds! But the ungodly do so well, and all my prayers have got me nowhere.

8. Friend: Now, dear friend, be careful – this is blasphemy. Who are you to go against the wise decrees of heaven?

(9–12 are missing or fragmentary.)

13. Sufferer: Oh it's no use! I shall throw it all up – my home, my god, the lot – and take to the road.

(14 is fragmentary. A surviving phrase, 'Human activity, which you do not want . . .', suggests a rebuke for this opting out of society and of family responsibilities.)

15. Sufferer: Families can turn against you – everything's a gamble.

(16 is fragmentary. Its opening words, 'Humble and submissive one . . .', perhaps imply an appeal to the protester to be his real self again.)

17. Sufferer: Everything's upside down now – princes in rags, beggars well dressed – what can you do?

(18 and 19 are fragmentary.)

20. Friend: Your subtle mind has led you astray. Goodness does succeed; piety does bring blessing.

21. Sufferer: And rogues and cheats make their pile!

22. Friend: Your rogue will pay for it! Now get right with your god, and what you have lost in a whole year you

will make up in a moment.

23. Sufferer: Life isn't like that! A father slaves, his son lies around. One brother shines, the other fails. As for one's god – I did bow to him, and what happened? I'm bowing to everyone now!

24. Friend: This is clever talk, but it's arrogant. These inequalities are the pattern of life, and a greater mind than ours has willed them.

25. Sufferer: But you don't get my point. It's not only that some get on and others don't. It's that the way to get on is to be wicked; the way to get no pity is to need it.

26. Friend: I'm afraid that's human nature, and that is how the gods saw fit to make us – incurably crooked. There, like it or not, is your answer.

27. Sufferer: You are kind, good friend! Sympathize, and help me. And may my personal god and goddess, who have cast me off, show mercy. For there is Shamash (above), the shepherd of the nations!

So the Theodicy, unlike 'Man and his God', or 'Ludlul', does not see suffering as necessarily penal. In relation to the book of Job we may be struck by the fact that here, as there, the conversation is largely at cross purposes – the sufferer dominated by what he observes; the friend, by what he believes. But there are two points in particular where the two works are poles apart. First, in stanza 13, where this sufferer moves from protest to revolt:

I will ignore my god's regulations and trample on his rites.

This was exactly what the Satan had tried and failed to bring about in Job.

Secondly, in stanza 26 the friend in his final speech makes heaven not merely suffer man's perversity but actually implant it, aware of all the misery it would entail:

Narru, king of the gods, who created mankind,
And majestic Zulummar, who pinched off the clay for
    them,
And goddess Mami, the queen who fashioned them,
Gave twisted speech to the human race.
With lies, and not truth, they endowed them forever.

So indeed it has turned out – as human values demonstrate:

137

Solemnly they speak favourably of a rich man,
"He is a king", they say, "riches should be his",
But they treat a poor man like a thief,
They have only bad to say of him and plot his murder . . . .[1]

So the gods have it both ways. In clemency they may rescue a worshipper from demons and from his fellow men (and in the poem's final line we are reminded of Shamash the guardian of justice); yet it was their decision that man should not encroach upon their prerogatives: either of immortality (as Gilgamesh was made aware)[2] or of justice.

'Tomorrow we die'

The brevity of life, and the shadow it casts over all our hopes and aims, is faced not only in Ecclesiastes but in various other writings of the ancient Near East. Here we sample two texts which recommend enjoyment of life's good things while we have them, and a third which – with wry humour – questions whether anything at all is worth the trouble of pursuing.

The Song of the Harper[3]

Various Egyptian tombs are decorated with the picture of a funeral feast, at which a harper sings a song on the theme of life and death, in terms which apparently remained broadly the same over many generations. The extract below is from a papyrus of *c.*1300 BC, but the poem professes a much earlier origin.

After dwelling on the transience of life, and the decay of men's possessions ('their walls are broken apart, and their places are not'), the singer bids us take our minds off what awaits us all.

Follow thy desire, as long as thou shalt live.
Put myrrh upon thy head and . . . fine linen upon thee . . .

Let not thy heart flag.
Follow thy desire and thy good.
Fulfil thy needs upon earth, after the command of thy
    heart,
Until there comes for thee that day of mourning . . .

---

[1]*ANET*[3], p.604; *cf. BWL*, p.89.   [2]See below, p.139.
[3]Text in *ANET*, p.467.

If this calls to mind what Ecclesiastes advocates from time to time, the following ancient Mesopotamian text is closer still.

Siduri's Advice to Gilgamesh[1]

In his grief at the death of his heroic friend Enkidu, king Gilgamesh has set out to find the secret of immortality. Reaching at last the garden of the gods he encounters the woman Siduri, the wine maker, but she has this to tell him:

> Gilgamesh, where are you making for?
> You will never find the life you seek!
> When the gods created man,
> It was death that they allotted him,
> While life they kept in their own hands.
> As for you, Gilgamesh, fill your belly,
> Make merry, day and night!
>
> Let your clothes be sparkling fresh,
> Your head washed, your body bathed.
> Give thought to the child whose hand is in yours,
> And let your wife delight in your embrace!
> These things are the human lot.

In Ecclesiastes 9:7–9 we read:

> Go, eat your bread with enjoyment, and drink your wine with a merry heart; for God has already approved what you do.
> Let your garments be always white; let not oil be lacking on your head.
> Enjoy life with the wife whom you love, all the days of your vain life which he has given you under the sun, because that is your portion in life . . . .

For comments on this strand in Qoheleth's teaching, see above, pp.100ff., 111ff.

The Dialogue of Pessimism, or The Obliging Servant

Whether this lively text is meant to entertain us or unsettle us – or both – the attitude to life which it depicts is one of airy inconsequence and idle disillusion. Ecclesiastes' catch-

---

[1] *Cf. ANET*, p.90a. The Gilgamesh Epic, from the 3rd millennium BC, is most fully preserved in a 7th-century text from the library of King Asshurbanipal of Nineveh.

word, 'Vanity of vanities!' or, 'Meaningless! Meaningless!', could be its motto; but it says it with a shrug and a yawn, not a shudder. And unlike Ecclesiastes it gives no hint that such a motto might *not* after all be the last word on the subject or 'the end of the matter'.

The exchanges begin quite unannounced, as cross-talk between a vacillating master and a quick-witted servant who, with a straight face, congratulates him on every whim and counter-whim – and finally has the last thrust.

What follows here is not a translation,[1] but a very free paraphrase to bring the conversation as close as possible to our own idiom. For fullness and accuracy the translations mentioned in the footnote should be used.

'Here, slave!' 'Sir?' 'The chariot – I'm off to the palace.' 'Fine, sir, you'll be in their good books.'

'No, I'll not go after all.' 'Sir, don't on any account. The king might send you off to the back of beyond. A real bed of nails he'd give you!'

'Slave!' 'Sir?' 'Get me ready for dinner, and be quick about it.' 'Dinner, sir, of course. Expands the mind! It's kind of religious too.'

'No, I don't feel like it now.' 'How right, sir; you're above these routine things!'

(Next there are plans to go hunting – or not! – and talk of becoming a family man, and thoughts of a lawsuit – or of dropping it. [The text seems disordered at this point.])

Now for something daring:

'Slave!' 'Sir?' 'I'm taking the law into my own hands!' 'But of course, sir! It's the only way to make ends meet.'

'No, no. I shall do nothing of the kind.' 'Well, they'd have flayed you alive, sir, if they'd caught you!'

'Slave!' 'Sir?' 'I feel in the mood for love.' 'Ah, nothing like it, sir, for taking your mind off things!'

'Oh, I don't feel like it now.' 'And what is woman, sir, but a trap, a hole, a ditch, a dagger!'

'Slave!' 'Sir?' 'Water for my hands – I shall offer a sacri-

[1]The text is translated in, *e.g.*, *ANET*, p.438 (R. H. Pfeiffer); *BWL*, pp.145–149 (W. G. Lambert); *ANET*[3], p.601 (R. D. Biggs). Lambert suggests a date towards the end of the Cassite period (*c.*1200 BC) at the earliest (*BWL*, p.141).

fice.' 'That's right, sir, it's a good bargain. Get the god in your debt!'

'No, after all ...' 'Sir, that's the idea! Keep your god guessing. You can teach him to run after you like a dog.'

(Next there is talk of moneylending. Very profitable, says the servant. Mind you, very risky.) Then a grand gesture:

'Slave!' 'Sir?' 'I will do a good deed for my country!' 'Very sound, sir! Even Marduk will take notice.'

'No. On second thoughts ...' 'Right again, sir! What does it come to? Have a look at the skulls on the ruin heap! Can you tell which was which? – the public nuisance or the public benefactor?'

(Finally he toys with a serious question):

'Slave!' 'Sir?' 'Tell me – what is *good*?' 'Oh, to be dumped in the river, both of us, with our necks broken! It's no use having grand ideas of ourselves.'

'No, slave, I'll kill you and send you on ahead.'

'And would my master survive even three days – without me to look after him?'

Opinions differ over the intention of this piece. Is it propaganda for nihilism, or simply an entertainment? Or perhaps a satire to show up the fatuous rich over against the canny underdog? However light the touch, the fact remains that the comedy – if such it is – is 'black', knocking everything within range off its pedestal, whether it be king or country, god or good. If 'jesting Pilate' earned his epithet reluctantly by his defensive retort, 'What is truth?', this writer throws out the question, 'What is good?' with a flourish. The answer is gratuitously cynical, and it makes little difference whether it is said in bitterness or in jest.

Ecclesiastes, too, is bitter; but by contrast it is never cynical, nor ever flippant. And, as we have seen, the blackness of what (in the author's words) *'I saw'* does not succeed in quenching the tiny spark of *'Yet I know ...'*[1] – a spark of overt conviction whose logical outcome is the confident glow of the epilogue to that book.

[1]Ec. 8:12; *cf.* 3:12,14; 11:9.

141

Appendix B

Ecclesiasticus, or
The Wisdom of Jesus son of Sirach

The title and author

Ecclesiasticus (often abbreviated as Ecclus.) was a title borrowed by Jerome from the Old Latin Bible, perhaps reflecting the popularity the book enjoyed in the early church. In the Septuagint it was known more accurately by the alternative title above, which is usually shortened to Sirach (the Greek form of Sira) or to Ben (= son of) Sira.

The author was a teacher, widely travelled (34:11–12; 51:13), who set up his 'school' (51:23) either literally or in the form of his book, which he wrote early in the 2nd century BC – say, 190–180. Only about two-thirds of it survive in Hebrew, recovered since 1896 in miscellaneous manuscripts from the *genizah* or lumber-room of an ancient synagogue in Cairo, plus some subsequent finds at Qumran and Masada. For the complete text we are indebted to Ben Sira's grandson, who translated it into Greek in 132 BC for the benefit of his fellow Jews in Egypt, as he tells us in the Prologue. It is this Greek version which RSV translates, referring in footnotes to the Hebrew where this is extant.

Traditional Wisdom

In general, Ben Sira's style and outlook are those of the book of Proverbs. He has the same motto, 'To fear the Lord is the beginning of wisdom' (1:14), and his opening poem on Wisdom's role in creation brings Proverbs 8 at once to mind. He addresses the reader as 'my son' in his early chapters, encourages his faith ('who ever trusted in the Lord and was put to shame?', 2:10), and showers him with the do's and don'ts of wisdom in the imperative mood, as well as with the pithy comments on life which put wisdom into the indicative, in the manner of traditional sentence-sayings – although there is more thematic grouping here than in the earlier book.

All the favourite topics of Proverbs are here, often memorably presented. On the use of words, for instance,

A slip on the pavement is better than a slip of the tongue.
20:18.

On the fool,

Mourning for the dead lasts seven days,
but for a fool or an ungodly man it lasts all his life.
22:12.

On friends,

Let those that are at peace with you be many,
but let your advisers be one in a thousand.
6:6.

– and so on, praising the pursuit of wisdom, the training of children, generosity, chastity, hard work; all within the framework of faith in God.

Naturally Ben Sira has his own angles on the subjects he shares with Proverbs, adding fresh insights or caveats, or airing some prejudices. He has grave reservations, for example, on *the world of business*:

A merchant can hardly keep from wrongdoing,
and a tradesman will not be declared innocent of sin.
26:29.

As a stake is driven firmly into a fissure between stones,
so sin is wedged in between selling and buying.
27:2.

He agrees with Ecclesiastes on the subject of *wealth*, that it is not all joy; for it brings worries to its owners – and not only worries, he adds, but temptations which few can resist (31:1–11). Among these is the urge to treat people as means to one's ends (13:5–7):

he [the rich man] will drain your resources
and he will not care.
When he needs you he will deceive you,
he will smile at you and give you hope . . .
and finally he will deride you.

'Riches are good', admittedly, 'if they are free from sin' (13:24) – but to Ben Sira it is evidently a big 'if'.

Likewise a *woman* is, to him, a very mixed blessing: potentially God's most precious gift (26:13–18; 36:22–26), but an endless worry as a daughter (42:9–11) and a death-trap as a charmer (9:1–9; 42:12–13). He even dares to say:

> Better a man's wickedness
> than a woman's goodness.
>
> 42:14, NEB.

On the prospect of *death*, and an uninviting Hades (14:16), he is spurred like Qoheleth to make the most of life:

> Do not deprive yourself of a happy day.
>
> 14:14.

– yet he improves on Qoheleth by preceding this advice with

> Do good to a friend before you die,
> and reach out and give him as much as you can.
>
> 14:13 (*cf.* 17:25–30).

He also appears to see one's day of death as God's day of reckoning, potent enough to balance the accounts of a lifetime.

> Even on the day a man dies it is easy for the Lord
> to give him his deserts.
> One hour's misery wipes out all memory of delight,
> and a man's end reveals his true character
>
> 11:26–27, NEB (*cf.* 18:24).

Hence the famous saying,

> Call no one happy before his death.
>
> 11:28.

Hence too, more practically,

> In all you do, remember the end of your life,
> and then you will never sin.
>
> 7:36.

In one minor respect Ecclesiasticus stands closer to foreign didactic writings than to those of Israel, by including a passage on the merits of different *trades*.[1] Predictably it is

---

[1] *Cf.* the Egyptian text 'In Praise of Learned Scribes', *ANET*, pp.431f., and 'The Satire on the Trades', *ANET*, pp.432–434.

the scribe's profession which surpasses the rest (38:24 –
39:11), even that of the physician (38:1–15).[1]

Wisdom and the chosen people

Ecclesiasticus differs from its predecessors chiefly in the
prominence it gives to Israel, her institutions and her history. This comes out in several ways:

a. Wisdom, although her scope is universal, has found no
resting-place except, by God's decree, in Israel and at
Jerusalem.

> In the holy tabernacle I ministered before him,
> and so I was established in Zion.
>
> 24:10 (1–12).

b. Wisdom is identified with the Torah. After her account
of her exalted being (from eternity to eternity, 24:9) and her
life-giving benefits ('Come to me, . . . and eat your fill of my
produce', 24:19), we read:

> All this is the book of the covenant . . . ,
> the law which Moses commanded us
> as an inheritance for the congregations of Jacob.
>
> 24:23.

c. The climax of Ecclesiasticus comes in its six chapters of
the 'famous men' of Old Testament history (chs. 44 – 49),
crowned by a panegyric (50) on the recent High Priest
Simon ben Onias and on the splendour of his worship.

All this is very different from the way the canonical wisdom books play down the special relationship of Israel with
the LORD, to concentrate chiefly on man as man, under God
as Creator. But this is a difference of degree rather than of
kind. Ben Sira's 51 chapters are packed with universal sayings, far in excess of his particularly Israelite ones; while
the canonical books for their part are as concerned as he is –
for all their reticence – with the one true God, whose name
is Yahweh (as Proverbs and the narrative of Job bear witness), and whose 'commandments' give specific content to
Qoheleth's final call to fear him.

---

[1]RV, only slightly modified by RSV, produces an unfortunate but amusing
anticlimax at 38:15, 'He that sinneth before his Maker, let him fall into the
hands of the physician.' The context, however, makes it clear that this is
not his fate but his good fortune!

Ecclesiasticus and the canon

This book, along with The Wisdom of Solomon and the other Apocryphal or 'Deutero-Canonical' writings, falls outside the Hebrew canon of Scripture, and is therefore defined in (for example) the Anglican confession as one of the books which 'the Church doth read for example of life and instruction of manners; but yet doth it not apply them to establish any doctrine'.[1]

On 'life and manners' (or, as we should say, conduct), the samples we have taken may well encourage us to explore Ben Sira's wit and wisdom further. We have said nothing, for instance, of his eloquent anticipation of the gospel's denial of forgiveness to the unforgiving (28:1–7), or of the question, 'Shall we continue in sin, that grace may abound?', with his stunning rebuke in 5:4–7.

Yet there are moments when he lapses from his high level. For example, among his firm but fair and sensitive maxims on the treatment of a servant there comes the sickening remark,

> and for a wicked servant there are racks and tortures.[2]
>
> 33:26.

On another topic, many heartaches must have been inflicted by the sweeping estimate in 22:3b,

> and the birth of a daughter is a loss

– even when one takes into account the almost comic pessimism of 42:9–11, where the father worries himself to insomnia with daughter-shaped forebodings. And we have already quoted his jaundiced view of womanly goodness (p.144). Even if he spoke there as the victim of some do-gooder, he need not have complained elsewhere in the tones of Adam:

> From a woman sin had its beginning,
> and because of her we all die.
>
> 25:24.

Finally, as a potential source of doctrine, Ecclesiasticus may

[1] Article VI of the 39 'Articles of Religion', 1562, Book of Common Prayer.
[2] But see verse 29: 'Do not act immoderately toward anybody'; and verse 31, 'If you have a servant, treat him as a brother'. *Cf.* 7:20–21. So J. G. Snaith has reason to consider the racks and tortures metaphorical (*Ecclesiasticus*, p.164). At 23:10, however, the torture is clearly literal, and no rarity, which tells against metaphor in our verse.

have some responsibility for one of the tenets of Judaism where it diverges from Christianity over man and salvation. Ben Sira takes the view that God created everything in pairs of opposites:

> Good is the opposite of evil,
>   and life the opposite of death;
>   so the sinner is the opposite of the godly.
> Look upon all the works of the Most High;
>   they likewise are in pairs, one the opposite of the other.
>
> 33:14–15 (*cf.* 42:24).

This extends to the opposite tendencies within man (as formulated in later Judaism) towards good and evil, the *yēṣer ha-ṭôḇ* and the *yēṣer hā-rā'*. Although at one point Ben Sira laments the latter,

> O evil imagination, why were you formed . . .?
>
> 37:3.

he regards man nevertheless as perfectly capable of achieving goodness:

> It was (the Lord) who created man in the beginning,
>   and he left him in the power of his own inclination (*yēṣer*).
> If you will, you can keep the commandments,
>   and to act faithfully is a matter of your own choice.
> He has placed before you fire and water:
>   stretch out your hand for whichever you wish.
> Before man are life and death,
>   and whichever he chooses will be given to him.
>
> 15:14–17.

Admittedly the aim of this passage is to answer the excuse, 'Because of the Lord I left the right way' (15:11); and in the quotation of 33:14–15, above, the pairs of opposites in God's creation are used as analogous ('likewise') to those that are found in the moral realm. Perhaps the analogy should not be pressed, for when he says elsewhere that 'good things were created for good people, just as evil things for sinners' (39:25), he explains this by speaking of the use and misuse that people make of God's gifts (27), and by citing God's own employment of destructive forces as tools of judgment (28ff.). 'For all things will prove good in their season'(34).

But Ben Sira's thought is tending towards that of Jewish orthodoxy, which in the words of a modern exponent 'denies the existence of original sin, needing a superhuman counterweight . . . . True, the idea that the sin of Adam had brought death on all mankind is not unknown in Jewish teaching, but the reference is invariably to physical death, and is not to be confused with the spiritual death from which in Christian doctrine none can be saved except through faith in the risen Saviour. Man can therefore achieve his own redemption by penitence . . . .'[1]

This view in Ecclesiasticus of, in Gordis's phrase, 'free-will *without modification*'[2] (his italics), probably had to lead to self-redemption. What is clear is that could not lead, except by some unusually circuitous route, to the New Testament doctrine of salvation.

[1] I. Epstein, *Judaism* (Penguin Books, 1959), p.142.
[2] R. Gordis, *Poets, Prophets and Sages*, p.181.

Appendix C

The Wisdom of Solomon

Title and provenance

The title, however it arose, reflects accurately enough the chosen standpoint of the author, but it should be remembered that he makes no mention of his hero's name anywhere in the book. Just as Qoheleth, in Ecclesiastes, wears briefly the mantle of Solomon in order to explore the experiences that only such a king could command (yet leaves him unnamed), so this anonymous author makes himself the same king's mouthpiece. This time, however, it is not Solomon the hedonist, but the Solomon who set his heart on wisdom, who is made to speak to us.

The author is writing for people of Greek culture, as one who is fully at home in their language and thought-forms. He is clearly a loyal Jew of the Dispersion, possibly living in Alexandria, that centre of Hellenistic Judaism. His quoting of some parts of the Septuagint shows that he cannot be writing before about 200 BC at the very earliest, and scholars have tended to date his book late in the first century BC, paving the way for the more elaborate reclothing of Judaism in Greek dress by Philo (d. AD 45). D. Winston, however, proposes a date after AD 30 on linguistic and political grounds, making the author a contemporary and admirer (with reservations) of Philo. All datings alike rest on individual assessments of ambiguous evidence and can be no more than tentative.

The argument

One mark of Greek influence on this author is his orderly

unfolding of his theme, in contrast to his compatriots' preference for scattering their separate pearls of wisdom for the reader to pick up as he will. He opens with a call to the world's rulers to love righteousness, basing his appeal frankly on the character of the Lord and of the wisdom which proceeds from him,

> because wisdom will not enter a deceitful soul,
> nor dwell in a body enslaved to sin.
>
> 1:4.

He reinforces this by saying that in choosing evil one is forfeiting not only wisdom but life itself. Here he brings out his trump card, namely the prospect of either immortality (a major theme of the book) or final judgment.

This leads him to expound the destructive effects of the opposite philosophy, that death ends everything.[1] First there is likely to be hedonism, pathetic in its urgency –

> Let us crown ourselves with rosebuds before they wither
>
> 2:8 (6–9).

– but it will harden to a moral cynicism that knows no bounds:

> . . . let our might be our law of right.
>
> 2:11.

Moreover the natural target of this ruthlessness will be the man of principle, that 'inconvenient' figure (2:12) with his firm standards and high-flown claims. To Christian ears their reaction to him has almost the ring of prophecy:[2]

> He . . . boasts that God is his father.
> Let us see if his words are true . . .
> for if the righteous man is God's son,
> he will help him, and will deliver him . . .
> Let us test him with insult and torture . . .

---

[1]While the extreme followers of Epicurus are the most likely subject of this portrait, the language of 2:1–5 is strongly reminiscent of Ecclesiastes, to which this chapter is sometimes considered a counterblast. But the violent hedonism of verses 6ff. is so unlike Qoheleth's praise of simple pleasures that the revellers here are best seen as making Ecclesiastes their excuse rather than their pattern.

[2]But *cf.* also Glaucon's picture of a just man's fate in an unjust world: 'scourged, racked, fettered, blinded, and at last . . . crucified' (Plato, *The Republic*, Bk. II; *cf.* Everyman Edn., p.39). (On D. Winston's dating of Wisdom in the late thirties AD, 'prophecy' would again be the wrong term to use.)

> Let us condemn him to a shameful death,
> for, according to what he says, he will be protected.
>
> 2:16–20.

But the sceptics' fallacy lies in their first assumption, for death is not the end. As for the righteous,

> In the eyes of the foolish they seemed to have died . . .
> (but) their hope is full of immortality . . . .
> They will govern nations and rule over peoples . . .
>
> 3:2,4,8.

while as for the rest,

> the ungodly will be punished as their reasoning deserves . . .
>
> 3:10.

These great reversals occupy further chapters, with moral arguments against the way men judge success (*e.g.*, by quantity instead of quality, 3:13–14; 4:7ff.) and with dramatic foretastes of the final judgment, when the persecutors will see at last the truth about themselves—

> We fools! So it was we who strayed from the way of truth . . .
>
> 5:4,6.

– and when the Lord 'will arm all creation to repel his enemies' (5:17).

So the author appeals again to rulers to face their high responsibility,

> For the lowliest man may be pardoned in mercy,
> but mighty men will be mightily tested.
>
> 6:6.

They must set their hearts on wisdom (which now takes the centre of the stage again) if they would win an everlasting kingdom:

> Honour wisdom, that you may reign for ever.
>
> 6:21.

For their benefit, then, King Solomon (in whose name, it now emerges, the author writes) describes in chapters 7 – 9 how he found wisdom: not by attainment but by gift:

> For she is . . . a pure emanation of the glory of the Almighty.
>
> 7:25.

> . . . and I desired to take her for my bride.
>
> 8:2.

So in chapter 9 he records his prayer for such a gift, elaborating on the response he made at Gibeon (1 Ki. 3:5ff.) to God's 'Ask what I shall give you'.

The second half of the book (10 – 19) is devoted to showing, first, how wisdom guided the earliest men of God; secondly, how wisely and judiciously God dealt with the godly and the ungodly at the Exodus and Conquest; thirdly, how foolish and fatal it is to worship anything but the Creator. It is the second of these themes which dominates the final chapters, interpreting God's miraculous judgments and disciplines with much ingenuity, and reaching the encouraging conclusion that

> . . . in everything, O Lord, thou hast exalted
>   and glorified thy people
> and . . . not neglected to help them at all times
>   and in all places.
>
> 19:22.

So the kings of the earth (we may infer) will be well advised to show their wisdom by avoiding the folly of those ancient kings who persecuted those whom God protects. But that is left, unsaid, to their good sense!

Some leading ideas

This book is an essay in apologetics, presenting the faith of Israel to the rulers of the Gentile world, and indirectly to its own adherents who are living in that alien culture. The culture is Greek, therefore the thought-forms are Greek as far as possible; yet the teaching is, in its main intention, Israelite and biblical.

1. *Wisdom* is the dominant concept, presented very much as in the book of Proverbs with its emphasis on wisdom's moral and religious dimensions, and with her portrayal in quasi-personal terms (here more as the bride than as the orator). But along with this, a quite different way of speaking brings to mind the Stoics' concept of the Logos, the rational principle which runs through all things and gives them their coherence. In the saying,

> The Spirit of the Lord has filled the world,
> and that which holds all things together
> knows what is said
>
> 1:7.

a Greek reader would hear biblical truth[1] in a familiar form. Again, in the famous list of wisdom's twenty-one attributes in 7:22–24, and in the ensuing verses, several terms are from a Stoic[2] or in some cases a Platonic background, though they are accompanied by others (notably 'holy' (22)) which point to the revealed character of God in Scripture, of whose goodness and glory wisdom is the image and radiance or reflection (*apaugasma*, 26). This last point is important, since wisdom, despite her representation as now a person, now a kind of energy, is inseparable from the action and self-expression of God, with whose 'word' and 'spirit' (9:1–2,17) she can be spoken of in synonymous parallelism. Even the Lord's miracles can be credited to her:

> She brought them [Israel] over the Red Sea . . .
> but she drowned their enemies . . .
>
> 10:18–19.

Among these adventurous ways of speaking, then, there were terms that beckoned Greeks towards the faith of Israel; but there were other terms that would reappear in the New Testament (whether independently or from this source) to speak of Christ, the truly personal wisdom, word, radiance,[3] image,[4] and only-begotten[5] of God, 'in whom all things were created' and 'all things hold together'.[6]

2. *Immortality* is prominent, not only in the well-known passage of 3:1 ff. on 'the souls of the righteous', but throughout the book. It can be used figuratively to speak of perpetuating one's name in the only worth-while way—

> for in the memory of virtue [not in one's offspring]
> is immortality
>
> 4:1.

[1]*Cf., e.g.,* Pr. 8:27–31; Je. 23:24; and, as later revealed, Col. 1:17.

[2]*Viz.,* 'intelligent', 'subtle', 'lively', 'beneficent' (*philanthrōpon*), 'she pervades and penetrates' and (8:1) 'orders'. For documentation on these and other terms in the passage, see D. Winston, *The Wisdom of Solomon,* pp.178–190.

[3]*apaugasma,* Heb. 1:3.   [4]*eikōn,* Col. 1:15.

[5]*monogenēs,* Jn. 1:18, *etc.;* but this adjective is used in its secondary sense of 'unique' in Wisdom 7:22.

[6]*Cf.* Col. 1:16–17 (but the verb for 'hold together' in Col. 1:17 is different from that of Wisdom 1:7).

– but that is the exception. Its literal sense is the rule. 'The righteous live for ever' (5:15), since death was not man's proper destiny:

> for God created man for incorruption . . . ,
> but through the devil's envy death entered the world,
> and those who belong to his party experience it.
>
> 2:23–24.

So, although immortality must be sought, and can be forfeited, it is God's willing gift to the righteous and the wise. 'Righteousness is immortal' (1:15), 'in kinship with wisdom there is immortality' (8:17); and God is the source of both:

> to know thee [God] is complete righteousness,
> and to know thy power is the root of immortality.
>
> 15:3.

On the other hand, the word 'resurrection' is never used here,[1] although the fact of it may well be implied in 3:7ff., speaking of the departed righteous:

> In the time of their visitation they will shine forth,
> and will run like sparks through the stubble.
> They will govern nations and rule over peoples . . .

This way of speaking is close enough to that of Daniel 12:2–3 and 7:27 to imply that in emphasizing the soul's immortality the writer has not lost sight of the kingdom to be set up on earth in the age to come, and the role of the departed saints within it.

In two places, however, he uses language that strongly suggests the Platonic view of man as a duality in which a pre-existent and immortal soul enters a body as its temporary dwelling.[2] Speaking for Solomon, he counts himself fortunate:

> As a child I was by nature well-endowed,
> and a good soul fell to my lot;
> or rather, being good, I entered an undefiled body.
>
> 8:19–20.

But he concurs with Plato on the down-drag of the physical,

---

[1] Contrast its confident use in 2 Macc. 7:14; 12:43–45.

[2] As D. Winston points out, however, he does not take up the Platonic notion of the transmigration of souls, nor the view that to be assigned (or indeed attracted) to a body implied that the soul in question was already 'fallen' (*The Wisdom of Solomon*, p.26).

though he stops short of treating it as the soul's tomb (*sōma* = *sēma*) or prison:

> for a perishable body weighs down the soul,
> and this earthly tent burdens the thoughtful mind.
>
> 9:15 (*cf.* Plato, *Phaedo*, 81c).

Opinions are divided as to his real position on this: whether he has accepted the Greek dualism of spirit and matter, or has accommodated only his language, not his theology, to the Greek view of life. But whatever allowances one makes for coincidences in descriptions of bodily limitations (after all, Paul also spoke of this 'earthly tent'), it needs special pleading to make the language of the former quotation (8:19–20) fit the biblical rather than the Platonic view of man.

3. On *Israel and the nations*, which is the theme of the second half of the book (10 – 19), the initial approach is to relate everything to Wisdom, distinguishing those who served her from those who passed her by (*e.g.*, 10:9,8). But soon it is God himself who dominates the story, and the conflict centres upon the 'holy people' and their oppressors at the Exodus. Here the apologetic motif develops three main thrusts: to show how reasonable were God's judgments and disciplines, how unreasonable is idolatry, and with what wise mastery of the elements God worked his miracles.

a. *His judgments* were reasonable in both senses of the word: in their aptness and their restraint. It was apt enough that those who worshipped animals should be plagued by them,

> that they might learn that one is punished
> by the very things by which he sins,
>
> 11:16.

and that the nation that had consigned infants to the river should find its waters turned to blood – whereas the righteous would find water in the very desert (11:1–14). Even so, the punishments were meted out with great restraint and patience, 'little by little' (11:20; 12:2,10), even upon the Canaanites, since God 'loves the living' and would give them 'a chance to repent' (11:26; 12:10). So the familiar objection that the God of Israel is harsh and partisan is warmly answered.

b. *Idolatry* is attacked roundly and at length for the folly of admiring the creation while ignoring the Creator; yet there is a momentary sympathy for even this:

> Yet these men are little to be blamed,
> for perhaps they go astray while seeking God . . .
> For as they live among his works they keep searching,
> and they trust in what they see,
> because the things that are seen are beautiful.
>
> 13:6–7.

However, the writer continues, this is really no excuse,

> for if they had the power to know so much
> that they could investigate the world,
> how did they fail to find sooner the Lord of these things?
>
> 13:9.

c. On *God's miracles* at the Exodus the argument is as far-fetched to modern ears as it was doubtless appealing in its time. It makes great play with God's manipulation of the elements – so that water lost its power over fire in the plague of hail (16:22b), and fire its power to give light in the plague of darkness (17:5), or to melt the snow-like manna (as the sun did) but to cook it instead (16:22a, 23; 19:21); and so on.

> For the elements changed places with one another,
> as on a harp the notes vary the nature of the rhythm,
> while each note remains the same.
>
> 19:18.

This analogy with the notes of the scale, re-ordered by the composer but not re-tuned, would be seen as answering the misgiving that miracles breach the rational order, while at the same time invoking the respectability of a well-known physical theory: that of Heraclitus on the transmutation of the elements.[1]

So the writer keeps in mind his non-Jewish readers right to the end, while vigorously affirming the special calling of those whom he ventures to describe as 'a holy people and blameless race' (10:15). Whether or not his book impressed the 'rulers of the earth' whom it apostrophized, it will certainly have fortified his friends against the cold winds of religious scepticism.

Conclusion

Enough has probably been said to show the main strengths

---

[1] *Cf.* C. Harris, in Gore's *New Commentary*, p.69.

and weaknesses of this appeal to the Greek-speaking and Greek-thinking world. Its achievement in meeting that world on its own ground meant that some of its arguments were doomed to perish along with the non-biblical presuppositions on which they rested (as in the section immediately above). Some of its language, too, especially in relation to the doctrine of man, concedes too much to dualistic views to make it a reliable theological guide. But its insistence that wisdom springs from God alone and dwells with godliness, that the righteous live and reign for ever, that the impenitent will be finally judged, and God's kingdom totally victorious, make it a heartening book to study. If the tortuous reasoning of the final chapters leaves the modern reader dazed and disappointed, nothing can detract from the eloquence of the rest. And it is arguable (as we have seen) that the New Testament may have drawn from this source some of its most striking expressions for the relation of the Son of God to the Father.

A short bibliography

General

W. Baumgartner in H. H. Rowley (ed.), *The Old Testament and Modern Study* (Oxford University Press, 1951), pp. 210–237.

J. L. Crenshaw, *Old Testament Wisdom: An Introduction* (John Knox Press, 1981; SCM Press, 1982).

J. L. Crenshaw (ed.), *Studies in Ancient Israelite Wisdom* (KTAV, New York, 1976).

J. A. Emerton in G. W. Anderson (ed.), *Tradition and Interpretation* (Oxford University Press, 1979), pp. 214–237.

J. G. Gammie *et al.* (eds.), *Israelite Wisdom* (Scholars Press, 1978).

R. Gordis, *Poets, Prophets and Sages* (Indiana University Press, 1971).

M. Noth and D. W. Thomas (eds.), *Wisdom in Israel and in the Ancient Near East* (Rowley Festschrift), *VTS* 3 (1955).

G. von Rad, *Old Testament Theology*, I (Eng. edn, Oliver and Boyd, 1962), pp. 418–459.

G. von Rad, *Wisdom in Israel* (Abingdon, 1972).

R. N. Whybray, *The Intellectual Tradition in the Old Testament* (*BZAW* 135, 1974).

J. G. Williams, *Those Who Ponder Proverbs: Aphoristic Thinking and Biblical Literature* (Almond Press, 1981).

Proverbs

W. F. Albright, 'Canaanite-Phoenician Sources in Hebrew Wisdom', *VTS* 3 (1955), pp. 1–15.

G. Boström, *Proverbiastudien: Die Weisheit und das fremde*

Weib in Sprüche 1 – 9 (Lund, 1934).

J. D. Crossan (ed.), *Gnomic Wisdom (Semeia* 17, 1980).

M. J. Dahood, *Proverbs and Northwest Semitic Philology* (Rome, 1963).

F. Delitzsch, *Proverbs* (T. & T. Clark, 1884).

E. Jones, *Proverbs and Ecclesiastes (Torch Bible Commentaries*, SCM Press, 1961).

C. Kayatz, *Studien zu Proverbien 1 – 9* (Neukirchener Verlag, 1966).

D. Kidner, *Proverbs (Tyndale Commentary*, IVP, 1964).

W. McKane, *Proverbs: A New Approach (Old Testament Library*, SCM Press, 1970).

H. Ringgren, *Word and Wisdom* (Lund, 1947).

W. M. W. Roth, *Numerical Sayings in the Old Testament (VTS* 13, 1965).

J. Ruffle, 'The Teaching of Amenemope and its Connection with the Book of Proverbs', *Tyn.B* 28 (1977), pp. 29–68.

J. C. Rylaarsdam, *Proverbs to Song of Solomon (Layman's Bible Commentaries*, SCM Press, 1964).

J. C. Rylaarsdam, 'The Proverbs' in *Peake's Commentary* (revised edn, Nelson, 1962).

G. Sauer, *Die Sprüche Agurs (BWANT* 84, 1963).

R. B. Y. Scott, *Proverbs, Ecclesiastes (Anchor Bible*, Doubleday, 1965).

P. Skehan, 'A Single Editor for the Whole Book of Proverbs', *CBQ Monographs* 1 (1971), pp. 15–26; reprinted in *SAIW*, pp. 329–340.

C. H. Toy, *Proverbs (ICC*, T. & T. Clark, 1899).

B. K. Waltke, 'The Book of Proverbs and Old Testament Theology', *Bibliotheca Sacra* 136 (1979), pp. 302–317.

R. N. Whybray, *Wisdom in Proverbs (Studies in Biblical Theology* 45, SCM Press, 1965).

Job

F. I. Andersen, *Job (Tyndale Commentary*, IVP, 1976).

M. Bič, 'Le juste et l'impie dans le livre de Job', *VTS* 15 (1966), pp. 33–43.

J. D. Crossan (ed.), *The Book of Job and Ricoeur's Hermeneutics (Semeia* 19, 1981).

A. B. Davidson, *Job (Cambridge Bible*, Cambridge University Press, 1893).

E. Dhorme, *Job* (Gabalda, Paris, 1926; Eng. edn, Nelson, 1967).

G. Fohrer, 'Zur Vorgeschichte und Komposition des

Buches Hiob', *VT* 6 (1956), pp. 249–267.

J. C. L. Gibson, 'Eliphaz the Temanite: Portrait of a Hebrew Philosopher', *SJT* 28[3] (1975), pp. 259–272.

R. Gordis, *The Book of God and Man* (University of Chicago Press, 1965).

R. Gordis, *The Book of Job* (Jewish Theological Seminary of America, 1978).

A. and M. Hanson, *Job* (*Torch Bible Commentaries*, SCM Press, 1953).

W. A. Irwin, 'Job' in *Peake's Commentary* (revised edn, Nelson, 1962).

H. Knight, 'Job (Considered as a Contribution to Hebrew Theology)', *SJT* 9 (1956), pp. 63–76.

R. Polzin and D. Robertson (eds.), *Studies in the Book of Job* (*Semeia* 7, 1977).

M. H. Pope, *Job* (*Anchor Bible*, Doubleday, 1973).

H. H. Rowley, 'The Book of Job and its Meaning', *From Moses to Qumran* (Lutterworth, 1963), pp. 141–183.

H. H. Rowley, *The Book of Job* (*New Century Bible*, Marshall, Morgan & Scott, 1976).

N. M. Sarna, 'Epic Substratum in the Book of Job', *HUCA* 37 (1966), pp. 73–106.

N. H. Snaith, *The Book of Job* (*Studies in Biblical Theology*[2], XI, SCM Press, 1968).

S. Terrien, *Job* (*Commentaire de l'Ancien Testament* 13, Delachaux et Niestle, 1963).

S. Terrien, 'Job', *The Interpreter's Bible*, 3 (Abingdon, 1954).

M. Tsevat, 'The Meaning of the Book of Job', *HUCA* 37 (1966), pp. 73–106; reprinted in *SAIW*, pp. 341–374.

C. Westermann, *The Structure of the Book of Job: a form-critical analysis* (Fortress Press, 1981).

Ecclesiastes

G. L. Archer, 'Ecclesiastes', *Zondervan Pictorial Encyclopaedia of the Bible*, 2 (1975).

G. A. Barton, *Ecclesiastes* (*ICC*, T. & T. Clark, 1908).

M. J. Dahood, 'Canaanite-Phoenician Influence in Qoheleth', *Biblica* 33 (1952), pp. 30–52, 191–221.

M. J. Dahood, 'Qoheleth and Recent Discoveries', *Biblica* 39 (1958), pp. 302–318.

F. Delitzsch, *Canticles and Ecclesiastes* (T. & T. Clark, 1891).

M. A. Eaton, *Ecclesiastes* (*Tyndale Commentary*, IVP, 1983).

K. Galling, *Prediger Salomo* (*Handbuch zum Alten Testament*, 18, 1940).

H. L. Ginsberg, 'The Structure and Contents of the Book of Koheleth', *VTS* 3 (1955), pp. 138–249.

R. Gordis, *Koheleth, the Man and his World* (Schocken, 1951).

G. S. Hendry, 'Ecclesiastes' in *New Bible Commentary* (IVP, ¹1953, ³1970).

H. W. Hertzberg, *Der Prediger (Kommentar zum Alten Testament*, 1963).

D. Kidner, *A Time to Mourn, and a Time to Dance (The Bible Speaks Today*, IVP, 1976); reissued as *The Message of Ecclesiastes (The Bible Speaks Today*, IVP, 1984).

A. Lauha, *Kohelet* (Neukirchener Verlag, 1978).

J. A. Loader, *Polar Structures in the Book of Qohelet* (de Gruyter, 1979).

O. Loretz, *Qohelet und der alter Orient* (Herder, 1964).

A. H. McNeile, *An Introduction to Ecclesiastes* (Cambridge University Press, 1904).

E. H. Plumptre, *Ecclesiastes (Cambridge Bible*, Cambridge University Press, 1885).

J. G. Williams, 'What does it profit a man?', *Judaism* 20 (1971), pp. 179–193; reprinted in *SAIW*, pp. 375–389.

A. G. Wright, 'The Riddle of the Sphinx', *CBQ* 30 (1968), pp. 313–334; reprinted in *SAIW*, pp. 245–266.

W. Zimmerli, 'Das Buch Kohelet – Traktat oder Sentenzensammlung?', *VT* 24 (1974), pp. 221–230.

International reflections on life

R. A. Caminos, *Late Egyptian Miscellanies* (Oxford University Press, 1954).

A. Erman, *The Literature of the Ancient Egyptians* (Methuen, 1927).

B. Gemser, 'The Instructions of Onchsheshonqy and Biblical Wisdom Literature', *VTS* 7 (1959), pp. 102–128.

S. R. K. Glanville (ed.), *The Instructions of Onchsheshonqy* (British Museum, 1955).

E. I. Gordon, *Sumerian Proverbs* (University of Pennsylvania, 1959).

K. A. Kitchen, *Ancient Orient and Old Testament* (Tyndale Press, 1966).

S. N. Kramer, 'Man and his God', *VTS* 3 (1955), pp. 170–182.

W. G. Lambert, *Babylonian Wisdom Literature* (Oxford University Press, 1960).

J. B. Pritchard (ed.), *Ancient Near Eastern Texts* (Princeton University Press, ²1955, ³1969).

D. W. Thomas (ed.), *Documents from Old Testament Times* (Nelson, 1958).

The Apocrypha

R. H. Charles (ed.), *The Apocrypha and Pseudepigrapha of the Old Testament*, 2 vols. (Oxford University Press, 1913).

E. G. Clarke, *The Wisdom of Solomon* (*Cambridge Bible Commentary*, Cambridge University Press, 1973).

J. Geyer, *The Wisdom of Solomon* (*Torch Bible Commentaries*, SCM Press, 1963).

C. Harris, 'The Wisdom of Solomon' in C. Gore *et al.*, *A New Commentary* (SPCK, 1928).

W. O. E. Oesterley, 'Ecclesiasticus' in C. Gore *et al.*, *A New Commentary* (SPCK, 1928).

J. G. Snaith, *Ecclesiasticus* (*Cambridge Bible Commentary*, Cambridge University Press, 1974).

D. Winston, *The Wisdom of Solomon* (*Anchor Bible*, Doubleday, 1979).

Index of Scripture references

Index of authors

General index